Evolve - Number Twenty-Five -

New Millennium WRITINGS

Winner of a Golden Press Card Award for Excellence

Celebrating 20 years of publishing, awarding, and encouraging those passionate and dedicated writers and poets who shine new light on the human condition and the intangible miracles with which life subtly overflows.

Edited by Alexis Williams Carr
who dedicates this issue

*To Julius McKenna Carr,
illuminating our life
with a new
glow.*

EDITOR & PUBLISHER
Alexis Williams Carr

CONSULTING EDITOR EMERITUS
Don Williams

CONTRIBUTING EDITORS AND SUPPORT
*Everette Bach, Marianne Chrystalbridge, Doris Ivie, Cathy Kodra, Travis
Ladonuel, Meagan Lowans, Alyssa Merka, Steve Petty, Nancy and Will
Rickenbach, Amber Roberts, Laura Still, Jeanne Tredup, and Justin Williams*

NONCONTEST SUBMISSIONS EDITOR
Elizabeth Petty

ARCHIVE WEBMASTER
Mark Plemmons

TYPESETTING, LAYOUT, COVER DESIGN,

WEBSITE DESIGN, & ASSOCIATE PUBLISHER
Brent A. Carr

ESTABLISHED IN 1996
*Special thanks to the Tredup family of Kenosha, WI, Rod Williams of Nashville, TN,
and John and Margie Richardson, of Seymour, TN, who were present at the birth.*

PUBLISHED ANNUALLY
by New Millennium Writings, Knoxville, TN
hello@newmillenniumwritings.org
www.newmillenniumwritings.org

TWICE-ANNUAL NMW WRITING AWARDS
*For official rules and guidelines of the NMW Writing Awards, and noncontest
submissions, please visit our website or see page 267 for entry details.*

ISSN: 1086-7678   ISBN: 978-1-944977-14-6   CPDA BIPAD NO. 89927

To Julius McKenna Carr,
illuminating our lives
and our world
with a new
glow,
a novel
imagination,
and undeniable grit
to fulfill his soul's purpose:

To Julius McKenna Carr,
illuminating our lives
and our world
with a new
glow,
a novel
imagination,
and undeniable grit
to fulfill his soul's purpose:

The onliness of living by experiencing.

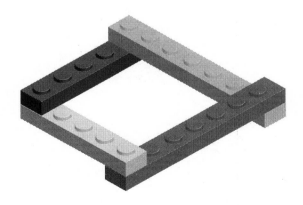

ABOUT NMW

FOR THE PAST 20 YEARS, we've been in the business of rewarding and publishing writers and poets. More than 1,600 emerging and established writers have graced *NMW's* pages, alongside interviews and profiles of the greatest writers of our time, including Ken Kesey, John Updike, Khaled Hosseini, and many others. *NMW's* distinctive vision, direction, and eye for marvelous writing have been shaped with the help of passionate guest judges, including Nikki Giovanni, David Madden, William Pitt Root, Maureen McLane, and Thea Gill.

New, emerging, established? All writing levels feel at home here! For example, of our most recent award winners, 75% had never won an award and 25% had never before been published. Our blind judging process levels the playing field and every submission receives a complete read-through, start to finish. May the most inspired storytelling prevail!

Recognizing and rewarding the voices of our time is an honor and a joy, and with your help we look forward to continuing this valuable work for decades to come.

Thank you and may your muse be inspired,

Alexis

OLSEN AND THE GULL

15

ERIC ST. CLAIR

INTRUDER

NOAH STETZER

24

39th Poetry Award

MEANWHILE, WE CALLED OURSELVES HUMAN,

28

CLAIRE BATEMAN

40th Poetry Award

THE PROPHET

ALEXANDER WEINSTEIN

32

40th Flash Fiction Award

THE MIRACLE IS TO WALK THIS EARTH

40

SHANNA YETMAN

39th Flash Fiction Award

KNIFE

JACKIE DAVIS MARTIN

46

39th Fiction Award

THE THINGS WE DID IN TEXAS 70

NINA VARELA
40th Fiction Award

INTO THE WORLD 92

KAREN HUNT
40th Fiction Award

HEARING SILENCE 114

SUSAN NATHIEL
39th Fiction Award

A PILGRIM UNAWARES 135

LINDA PARSONS

NATURAL REFLECTION 141

AN INTERVIEW WITH DON WILLIAMS

BRENT A. CARR

THE 25TH POETRY SUITE 185

41 SELECTED POETS AND FINALISTS

CONTENTS

New Millennium Writings, Issue 25, 2016, Evolve

Olsen and the Gull   15
Eric St. Clair—Short Fiction

Intruder   24
Noah Stetzer—Poetry*

Meanwhile, We Called Ourselves Human,   28
Claire Bateman—Poetry*

The Prophet   32
Alexander Weinstein—Flash Fiction*

The Miracle Is to Walk this Earth   40
Shanna Yetman—Flash Fiction*

Knife   46
Jackie Davis Martin—Fiction*

The Things We Did in Texas   70
Nina Varela—Fiction*

INTO THE WORLD   92
Karen Hunt—Nonfiction*

Hearing Silence   114
Susan Nathiel—Nonfiction*

A Pilgrim Unawares   135
Linda Parsons—Travel Essay

*First Place New Millennium Award Winner

THE NMW INTERVIEW

Natural Reflection: An Interview with *NMW* Founder, and Inspired Raconteur, Don Williams   141
  By Brent A. Carr

AWARD WINNERS & FINALISTS

Nonfiction   178
Poetry   179
Flash Fiction   180
Fiction   181
Competition Information   182

THE 25TH POETRY SUITE

Bowing to the Miniscule Tim Mayo   186
Early Warning Signs Sandy Longley   187
Elegy for a Bagful of Hearts Jo Christiane Ledakis   188
You Will Morph Patricia Barone   190
Hands Georganne Harmon   191
i forgot my poem today Mary Davies Cole   192
on the blued canvas and then... Linda Lee Harper   194
The Upright Piano Hedy Habra (non-contest selection)   196
In Lieu of a Christmas Letter, Ingrid Wendt   197
Under the Sign of Kronos Jim Glenn Thatcher   198
Specks in the Ointment Jim Glenn Thatcher   200
Chasmophile Berwyn Moore   202
What does it take Doris Ivie   203
Hic sunt dracones Annie Stenzel   204
To Christoforo Columbus Anca Hariton   205
Trainwreck, Minneapolis Arne Weingart   208
The Ice Storm Linwood Rumney   210

This Thing We Call Friendship... Barbara Mossberg 212

God Who Watches the Sparrows Laura Still 214

Fox Tracks Clarinda Harriss 215

Lady Alison Luterman 216

The Fisherman's Wife C. Ann Kodra 220

Field of Bullets, Medicine Bow Armin Tolentino 221

Miracle Lynne Burnett 222

River Swimming Shelley Kitchura Nelson 224

Born Lovers Out of Water Sashana Kane Proctor 226

An Epithalamium Robert A.B. Sawyer 228

Buddhist School of Cosmetology: Elaine Pentaleri 230

Saudade: 1983 Matt Hohner 232

How I Lost Your Poems Michael Morical 235

Meditation for Eggs Ellen LaFleche 236

Ferguson Emily Pittman Newberry 238

Walrus Robert S. Carr 239

The Milky Way in L.A. Keith Gaboury 240

SOFT Linda Parsons 241

Hesitating Fractions Cristina J. Baptista 242

Lawn Care Paul Beilstein 244

Crows Die Too Kevin McCarthy 246

Deuteronomy 23:2 Djelloul Marbrook 247

Dream Witness Marilyn Kallet 248

Fog Made of Iron Linda Nemec Foster 250

The Sultan's Tent Brandon Marlon 251

A Love Story Carolyn Evans Campbell 252

NOTES ON CONTRIBUTORS 257

mw

OLSEN AND THE GULL

Eric St. Clair

ONE HOT AFTERNOON, some five months after he had been cast away on the island, Olsen found out how to run the weather. A gull told him how.

There wasn't a thing on the island except gulls and their nests—millions of each—and the place was knee-deep with guano. Any other man, five months alone, hundreds of miles off the shipping lanes, might have gone crazy. Not Olsen, though. He lacked what it takes to go crazy with. He chased gulls by the hour, yelling at them because they could fly away any time they liked, while he couldn't—but he never talked to them in a conversational way. Nor did he talk to himself. Olsen, a man of few words and even fewer ideas, had nothing to say.

As a pastime, for amusement, he kicked the gulls' nests about, and trampled their eggs. True, the eggs were his sole food—but how he detested them! They were foul and rank and fishy, and the rainwater he sometimes found to drink them down with always reeked with guano. There were millions of eggs; gladly he trampled them! On this particular afternoon, Olsen trampled eggs in time to a chant he had made up, "Tromp, Tromp, Tromp!" and he was eggy up to his knees. He was neither sad nor happy about it; he just trampled and bellowed because it seemed the thing to do. A gray gull swooped down, landed, and stepped daintily toward him on its pretty little pink legs.

"Olsen," said the gull.

Olsen's bellowing died away. His trampling stopped. His mouth fell open. "Hoo?" he said. "Hawm? Now I have gone crazy."

"Very likely you have," said the gull. "But pull yourself together, Olsen. I propose to do you a favor."

Olsen's mind, never a quick one, remained motionless.

"You're a fine fellow, Olsen," the gull went on, "and we all think the world of you—but couldn't you be just a little more careful with our nests?" The gull eyed Olsen's eggy legs with some sort of expression: a gull's face being the type it is, it's hard to tell just what might be on its mind.

"Well, hey," said Olsen in his own defense. "If you—"

"What you need," the gull said, "is something to take your attention away from damaging our nests. Wholesome recreation."

"Burlesque shows!" breathed Olsen beatifically.

"Not quite," the gull said. "I have something different in mind. Now observe—" the gull hauled a length of stout twine from under its wing, "with this bit of twine (and the age-old wisdom I shall impart to you) you can build a cat's cradle that will raise the storm, or quiet it, whenever you feel like it. You can run the weather. My!" the gull said heartily, "won't that be fun!"

"I guess so," said Olsen. "But—"

"The power, Olsen! Think of it!" the gull cried ringingly. "The grandeur of the primeval storm! The roar of the white-crested seas that you can raise! The typhoon screaming, sheets of pelting grain, jagged lightning, the boom of thunder—at your call, Olsen!"

"No strippers?" said Olsen. "No fanny dancers?"

Not troubling to reply to this, the gull thereupon taught Olsen the art of constructing such a cat's cradle as would constrain the weather into obeying his, Olsen's, slightest whim. And Olsen found it sort of interesting. He tried a typhoon, a waterspout, a—but Olsen's mind was pretty limited. His slightest whim was indeed slight. He tried and tried, and after three days, he thought of doing some St. Elmo's Fire with his cat's cradle. Then his ideas ran out. The gulls, meanwhile, had been repairing nests, and laying new eggs. They hadn't much time for this, though, before Olsen got bored with the weather. One storm is pretty much like another, especially with a dull fellow like Olsen in charge—a spot of rain, a bit of wind, what's so wonderful about that?

He had been eating eggs right along, which the gulls did not apparently mind, but now that his storms had lost what charm they had had, Olsen noticed once more how bad the eggs tasted. Ugh! Bellowing the chant he had made up, "Tromp, Tromp, Tromp!" Olsen kicked nests right and left, and smashed many a fine egg.

"Olsen!" said the gray gull. "Oh, Olsen!"

"Tromp, Tromp, Tromp, Tromp."

"You stop that!" The way the gull said it made Olsen stop. "Really, Olsen," the gull said. "I can't figure you out. You're on an island paradise with the power of a god over the weather, a fine climate, plenty of good, nourishing food—"

"Food!" shouted Olsen. He caught up a nest full of eggs. "Lousy, stinking eggs!" He dashed the nest to the guano-covered rocks at his feet. "Fooey on such eggs!"

The gull gazed at Olsen in frank astonishment. "You mean," it said slowly, "you don't like our eggs?"

Olsen merely spat loudly on the nest he had smashed.

"If it's food you want," said the gull thoughtfully, "give me that twine."

Olsen did so, grinding the remnant of an egg under his heel.

"I am surprised," said the gull. "Why, we all like our eggs!"

Olsen was quite horrified. "You eat your own eggs?"

"On occasion, yes." Placidly, daintily, the gull worked with beak and claws. A truly wonderful cat's cradle took shape.

"CANNIBALS!" Olsen shouted.

"Oh, nonsense," said the gull. "Do pull yourself together, Olsen. Pay attention." It displayed the new cat's cradle, finished. "With this Wishing Pattern (which I will instruct you in making), you can command the sea to deliver any toothsome delicacy you want. For example, thus:" At once, the sea parted beside them. A hefty little oaken cask rolled to Olsen's feet.

"Me?" said Olsen, and the gull nodded. Whimpering with joy, Olsen caught up a stone. Drooling, he battered at the head of the cask. However, the cask turned out to contain what seemed to be a blend of gravel, worms, and various fish—all in a pretty well decomposed state. "Fool!" cried Olsen, shuddering at the smell.

"Well, my goodness, Olsen," said the gull fretfully. "Isn't there anything you like?" It pecked with gusto at what was inside the cask, making small cooing noises of pleasure. "Your very peculiar tastes are quite beyond me," the gull said after a time. "You must order for yourself from the sea. I will show you how."

Olsen would have made some comments on the diet of gulls, but words (as usual) failed him. Instead, he allowed himself to be taught how to build the Wishing Pattern cat's cradle. And now, whatever delicious foodstuff Olsen asked for, the sea would bring him. He scowled, as his mind churned slowly…what should he ask for…what did he want…?

This time, the gulls had almost a week of peace. They repaired old nests, they built new ones, they laid a thousand eggs. The happy period ended, though, for the same reason as before: Olsen was a man of no imagination whatever.

The Wishing Pattern cat's cradle worked just as the gull had said it would. Olsen got his hardtack and his salt pork and his tub of pineapple sherbet and his barrel of rum—and he settled down for an orgy. He gnawed at the hardtack and chomped the salt pork. He lapped up sherbet. He guzzled rum. But the salt pork turned out to be too salty. The hardtack jarred the back of his head when he gnawed it. The sherbet melted and ran. Only the rum really hit the spot—but even a lot of rum could not give Olsen any ideas for food other than what he was used to. Hardtack, salt pork, and pineapple sherbet were all he could think to ask for: hardtack, salt pork, and pineapple sherbet were what he got. Plus the rum, of course. So, when the week was up, here was Olsen back at work, kicking nests, trampling eggs, chanting his "Tromp, Tromp, TROMP!" Just like old times, except that the reek of rum was now added to the eggy stench of destruction.

"Olsen!" cried the gull almost in despair. "My good Olsen!" Olsen picked up an egg. He sighted at the gull.

"Please," the gull begged, preparing to dodge. "Have you no thought for the finer things the sea might bring you?"

"A keg of stale worms!" Olsen shouted. He hurled the egg, but missed widely (because of the rum in him).

"Olsen, my pet!" the gull wailed, as a gull wails when it feels bad. "My pride! My joy! My good fellow! Isn't there something…something…I don't know what you want; don't you know? Tell me! Anything to keep you from smashing our eggs! What, oh what, do you want?"

Olsen stood as though hypnotized by the gull's earnest gaze. After nearly a minute, a grin took over his face. "Women," he said.

"So!" said the gull. "The love of a good woman."

Olsen nodded eagerly, as this new idea of his slowly took over. The love of a good woman…He thought of the good women who stroll the streets of Buenos Aires, of Marseilles, of Singapore. He sighed noisily, and the rum in his head went round and round.

"I'm sorry, Olsen," said the gull. "I really am—but how could I call up a woman for you, out of the sea?"

"Easy!" cried Olsen. "Like this—" With two fingers in his mouth, he gave out a shrill wolf-call. And he stared about him, as if he really expected a woman to come in answer. Five months with no company but that of gulls had done things to what passed for Olsen's mind.

Pierced by the whistle, the gull shuddered. "Don't do that," it said. "But I'll show you how to make a Mermaid Line. Wouldn't a mermaid do, a lovely, lovely mermaid?" Coaxingly, the gull spoke.

"Mermaid!" sniffed Olsen. "Half fish, half girl! Why, how could I…" Olsen's voice trailed off as he scowled, trying to think. "Say…" he said after a bit. "Would I catch one just like I like?"

"You would!" the gull said. "She will be exactly what you ask for—so beautiful, and she will love you, Olsen!"

Grinning, Olsen gave back the Wishing Pattern, and the gull unraveled it.

"Observe," said the gull. "Over and under. Now reeve through the bight, so. Then you…"

Olsen, tongue a-dangle, followed each move of the gull's pink claws. After a couple of trials, no more than that, Olsen got it clear. (He was a sailor; even swimming in rum, he understood fancy ropework.)

"Now," said the gull, "toss one end into the sea." First, though, Olsen tied the line securely around his wrist. "But," said the gull, "what if—?"

"I don't take no chance she get away," said Olsen—and he threw the other end into the sea. It was a ten-foot line, intricate. Almost immediately the line quivered. Olsen had caught his mermaid. No need, though, to haul her in. Gladly, she leaped from the foam; willingly, she ran to him. Adoration swam wetly in her big blue-green eyes. Olsen threw back his head, and hollered with horror. With her mouth, the mermaid caught the line close to the knot around Olsen's wrist. She tugged impatiently. She must get back into the sea at once; this mermaid could not live on land. Still hollering, Olsen resisted the tug—but rum rolled and seethed inside his head, and his knees buckled. He recovered, and pulled desperately, straining against the pull of the mermaid. The line between them sang with tension—and suddenly parted. Olsen reeled, and fell heavily on a heap of guano behind him. The mermaid toppled backward into the sea. Her legs kicked briefly above the water before they sank. This mermaid had completely met

Olsen's specifications. She was half beautiful girl (the golden legs that Olsen had now glimpsed were a delight; the round, young hips a promise and a treasure) and half fish, from the waist on up; an unpleasant fish, like an outsize carp or a big herring. But now the fish part was under water, out of sight; only the lovely, lovely legs beckoned for a moment, and were gone. Olsen's mind was slow—but his instincts were in top working order. "You wait!" he bellowed, and rushed headlong toward the legs, into the sea. But the legs were gone—no, there they were, farther out. He floundered toward them. A wave caught him; he choked on the bitter water, and it almost sobered him. There were the legs again, though, in a new direction. Instinct conquered reason. Olsen splashed and struggled toward them. A wave swept over his head, but he came up undaunted. Now, suddenly, there was no bottom at all under Olsen's feet, and he could feel a current taking him to sea. A new instinct, self-preservation, spoke up. "Swim, Olsen," it counseled, but Olsen, of course, could not swim. The golden legs flashed close beside him, and disappeared. And something underneath the water grasped his ankle lovingly and gently. Olsen began again to holler as he felt himself being pulled under, gently, lovingly, but very firmly. After his hollering stopped, there were bubbles. Then the bubbles floated away.

The gull had watched all this with great interest. "What a remarkable mating custom!" it said to no one in particular. "Olsen is certainly a peculiar fellow."

It forgot about Olsen then, and set out looking for driftwood to patch up its nest.

"Olsen and the Gull" first appeared in *The Magazine of Fantasy and Science Fiction*, September 1964, Vol 27, No 3. Edited by Avram Davidson, Mercury Press, Inc.

The 39th

New Millennium Poetry Award

Noah Stetzer

INTRUDER

Noah Stetzer is a graduate of The MFA Program for Writers at Warren Wilson College and also a scholarship recipient from the Lambda Literary Retreat for Emerging LGBT Writers, and the Bread Loaf Writer's Conference.

He lives in the Washington, D.C. metro area.

CREATIVE CONSTRAINTS ARE OF great interest to me. I think because I'm suspicious of my own decision-making when crafting poems, I'm drawn to constraints because they give me some third-party tension against which I can compose—or they provide a distraction to kind of shut me up enough to maybe write something worthwhile. I can overwrite in the same way that as a kid I would over-explain if I thought I had done something wrong—that feeds my suspicion that when I'm writing I'm doing something wrong. As a medium, language is not like paint—language is this already-made construction that I then again manipulate into a poem... that sounds like a kind of appropriation, and I find that compelling and provocative and transgressive. Poetry reintroduces words to me as if I hadn't known them before, but I have, just not in the way that I'd thought. It's like when, as a kid, I saw my fifth-grade teacher at the supermarket, out of the context of my grade school classroom; suddenly she was so much more, and stranger, than how I had come to know her.

—Noah Stetzer

INTRUDER

Noah Stetzer

There are sixteen pills on the table, but today is the 12th which means
there ought to be eighteen pills because this month has thirty days, and I
make sure that the bottle has as many pills as days of the month,
every month, on the first of the month. And cause today is the 12th
and there are thirty days with eighteen days left there needs to be eighteen
pills—but there are only sixteen. And I check cause I have a system
of marks and calendars with red ink and lots of math that shows that I
forgot a pill or a mark or both or maybe neither or added
wrong back when I filled the bottle, or just forgot altogether cause
last night I was distracted, and so now I'm worried if one missed pill
might be enough, like maybe a line of a crack has surfaced along
the side of my face, where something's just a little broken or starting
to break. Because last night the knife went missing, or at least that's when I
couldn't find it, the knife I noticed missing after dinner when I
went to load the dishwasher. No big knife in the sink, not the knife drawer,
and nowhere else in the kitchen and my first thought was it was in the hand
of an intruder, all in black behind the closed guest room door waiting
for a moment, like now during the empty afternoon, when my guard
is down, and I'm alone in the house. Someone holding the missing knife,
making no noise, not moving: all night. But last night in the kitchen, I

thought, "you're crazy" and then, that I'd slipped the knife into my red backpack,
that I had the knife in my bag in case I needed it. That maybe
I'd packed the knife and then forgot, which makes sense but needs fixing because
I'd been forgetting things more, and what if I have started to forget
big things like this knife in my backpack? Cause I can see needing a knife.
I went to finish clearing this table and wiped off the crumbs and I
folded the cloth so I could go check my red backpack in the guest room
closet and did not find the missing knife there with my just-in-case clothes
and a week's worth of meds. And so today what's upsetting is the one
pill too many or one pill off depending on how you are looking
at it, and the extra pill that I may have taken or forgotten
to take. More upsetting is that I can't account for it either way,
which worries me that something might could now, again, slip up and in.

New Millennium Poetry Award

Claire Bateman

MEANWHILE, WE CALLED OURSELVES HUMAN,

Claire Bateman's newest poetry collection, *Scape,* was released in 2016 from New Issues Poetry & Prose. She has taught at Clemson University, the Greenville Fine Arts Center, and various workshops and conferences.

She lives in Greenville, South Carolina.

*F*OR ME, WRITING DEMANDS *a combination of order and messiness. I find it helpful to maintain, as much as possible, a drama-free exterior life so that I can be attuned to the nuances of quiet internal shifts and noticings, both subtle and large-scale (messy). I also find it essential to keep a wild, overflowing notebook of jottings and sketches: images and phrases that float through my mind, parts of conversations I overhear, etc. I've learned that it works better for me to follow such fragments toward a sense of the whole, like creating a collage, rather than to start with a pre-decided topic and then strain to force out a poem about it. Of course, the most nourishing thing for any writer to do is to read widely and voluminously in the context of cultivating a compassionate, omnidirectional curiosity.*

—Claire Bateman

MEANWHILE, WE CALLED OURSELVES HUMAN,

Claire Bateman

having unblinked our eyes to an extravagance of middles,
the world *in medias res* from the get-go,
teeming, packed, where the song of matter was
the sound of everything not touching—
continental drift, the deaths of oceans,
moving plates on a molten core,
just a little prestidigitation on the part
of the phenomenal universe, with nothing
the same different as before.
Thus we aspired to be both inside and outside,
and so constructed patio kitchens and sun room gardens;
we cultivated disequilibrium,
relished rocking and being rocked—
if possible, we would have planted tree houses in boats—
just as we craved categories.
We: the living. You: the departed.
Do not cross line.
And always, we practiced purification

New Millennium Writings, Issue 25, 2016
© 2015 Claire Bateman

by soaking, abrasion, radiation, steam,
sonic bombardment, saturation in snow and darkness.
Ever recursive, we instructed our children to inquire,
Why is this night the same as every other night?
since from time immemorial
we'd distrusted our relationship with time,
having detected a certain tendency toward drift;
apparently, we'd been assigned to occur
gradually and all at once,
though any of us could have slipped through a needle's eye
merely by erasing all the emptiness between our atoms,
like the honeycomb spaces in stacked pearls.
And concerning the sizes of various infinities,
no limitation was ever ascertained.
And most of the world's passageways remained invisible to us:
incendiary after-trails of music inside the skull;
backtracings of remorse burrowing into the future.
And each of us would have chosen, over all other gifts,
to possess a resplendent singing voice:
there was that much glory within us pressing for release!
As well as grief, the universal solvent.
For who did not find themselves
at the center of everything flying equidistantly away?
No wonder we so easily fell into errors of transposition
and so exposed our wounds, bandaging everything else.
And it was evening and it was morning of the first day.
And everywhere our faces cast their penumbras
as we asked ourselves:
If it's not good to live in the past,
why are we here together?

New Millennium Flash Fiction Award

Alexander Weinstein

THE PROPHET

Alexander Weinstein is the director of The Martha's Vineyard Institute of Creative Writing. He is the author of the collection, *Children of the New World* (Picador 2016), and his short stories and translations have appeared in *Cream City Review, Notre-Dame Review, Pleiades, PRISM International, Rio Grande Review, Salamander, Sou'Wester, World Literature Today,* and other journals. He is the recipient of a Sustainable Arts Foundation Award, and his fiction has been awarded the Lamar York, Gail Crump, Hamlin-Garland, Lascaux, and New Millennium Prizes. He teaches Creative Writing at Siena Heights University and the University of Michigan. A graduate of Indiana University's MFA program and Naropa University's Jack Kerouac School of Disembodied Poetics, he has been working as a creative writing teacher and freelance editor, and leads fiction workshops in the United States and Europe. His fiction can be found at *www.alexanderweinsteinfiction.com.*

Learning how to nurture play and experimentation in my writing has been of great value to me. This idea of play is essential to my work. It's the urge to capture the very magic that brought me to writing in the first place—a love of language, of creating characters and fantastical settings, of exploring stories and being surprised by what they show me. As I've grown as a writer and pursued writing professionally (through an MFA program, and then in publishing and editing my work), the importance of play took a backseat for a while. I think this happens as part of the process of seeking publication and also in dealing with rejections. There's the pitfall of approaching art as a commodity rather than a process of expression. I've had plenty of rejected stories, near misses, etc., and the key for me has been learning how to grow from this process and strengthen my work while maintaining the joy of returning to the page. Interestingly, even success can end up limiting the risks we take as writers; there can be a fear of producing new work unlike previously published stories.

Given this, I've made it a goal to constantly remind myself to rejoice in the writing process and to take creative risks that bring me joy as an author. It's a process of returning to that state of wonder and excitement that led me to become a writer in the first place, a sort of childlike enthusiasm for the play that fiction writing can provide.

—Alexander Weinstein

mw

THE PROPHET

Alexander Weinstein

W E ALL FELT THE SAME way when we heard about The Prophet: skeptical, jaded, a stirring that longed to become awe. We wanted to know whether it was really true. Had he actually taught a group of fifty in Flagstaff to levitate? If so, where was the proof? And when he did it again, this time fully recorded and posted online, we studied the YouTube clip like forensic scientists. The comment section was filled with naysayers, and yet, in all caps with exclamation marks, user after user attested to witnessing the miracle. "I WAS THERE!!! HE HAS ARRIVED!!!!" We shook our heads. It was smoke and mirrors, we told one another, trick photography; you could do anything with a Mac.

We doubted our doubts.

After all, we were ripe for this. Many of us had spent nights pondering the universe, high on medicinal-grade marijuana. We were yogic radicals, weekend ayahuasceros, freethinkers who gave UFOs a second chance, and we prized our transcendental moments from meditation retreats and self-empowerment seminars, collecting our small illuminations like keepsakes. We'd longed for this, coveted it, but now, in the light of a living prophet who was teaching people to transmit electricity through their third eyes, we were hesitant.

Then he began appearing in even our most skeptical friends' Facebook feeds: "WATCH THIS VIDEO!" And there atop a rock in Sedona, along with the collected crew, he merged with the universe, his body disappearing for a full eight seconds before rematerializing. We watched the slightly crooked iPhone recording, the prophet's voice an indecipherable murmur, the electromagnetic crackling on the phone, and suddenly the rocks were empty and the videographer was saying *holy shit* for eight seconds before the group returned, seated in lotus, as solid as pre-transcendence.

We had to witness it for ourselves.

We took paid vacations, left jobs, closed the coffee shops where we worked, found babysitters for the week or, remembering our sunbaked dreams of youth, took the kids with us (why shouldn't they experience enlightenment?) and loaded

up our Subaru wagons, leaving the cul-de-sacs where our dreams of nirvana had given way to Netflix.

They'd already built the amphitheater by the time we arrived: a fifteen-acre clearing amid the foothills. Someone had trucked in a generator, another had donated microphones, and a devotee who owned a sanitation company had donated over a hundred Porta Potties. We crammed into the clearing, side by side, unfolding yoga mats and placing meditation cushions beneath us, burning sage and drinking from BPA-free bottles as we listened.

There he was, far in the distance, his high-pitched voice ringing through the afternoon sunlight. We'd heard similar instructions in our YMCA yoga classes, Pilates workshops, and Reiki certification courses, but the presence of the prophet changed us. We felt our bodies glowing; we breathed in light; we discovered gravity wasn't a law, simply a habit we could kick; and there, in the holy cathedral of Flagstaff, we learned to levitate.

We stayed on.

We imagined it would end badly. We'd grown accustomed to expect the worst: the police would arrive to arrest us, the National Guard would use gas, the government would send drones, the prophet would be assassinated, and when he was killed the world would end. But none of that occurred. Instead we learned to place our hands on our neighbors' temples and free them from suffering, we healed wounds of karmic incarnations, we delivered astral liberation to our parents sitting in their living rooms watching reports of us on TV. And when the gas in the generator ran out, we tapped into the reserves of our electrons and powered the microphones back on.

All who came were enlightened, and they were fed and loved, but eventually we grew tired. We yawned. We wanted coffee. We longed for things: a refrigerator, text messages, movie popcorn. Looking into the eyes of our lovers, we realized we could only ascend together for so long. Ultimately we needed to read a book or play online solitaire. We wanted to go home. And so we went home.

The prophet is still out there in Arizona. He welcomes visitors and stragglers, providing illumination to the few who have yet to receive it, and every now and again they'll do a news story on him. They report that crime is non-existent, that war is on its way out, that world hunger has been solved, and nobody's in as much of a rush anymore. But the truth is, whether you're carrying recycling to the curb or lifting it with your chi, there's still this everyday reality to deal with. This past Thanksgiving the prophet appeared on all the stations. There he was with his small handful of steadfast devotees, each of them in lotus, melting the snow around where they sat. They joined hands and produced a great luminous egg of light that lit up the heavens brighter than the Northern Lights. It was beautiful, we admitted; then we changed the channel with our minds.

New Millennium Flash Fiction Award

Shanna Yetman

THE MIRACLE IS TO WALK THIS EARTH

Shanna Yetman's fiction appears online at *Connotation Press* and the *Writing Disorder*. She is a 2014 recipient of Chicago's Individual Artist Grant. When not writing fiction or enjoying her family, she works as the Communications Coordinator for the Institute of Environmental Sustainability at Loyola University Chicago.

Read her other stories at *writershannayetman.weebly.com*.

Though the word limits (300-1000) may be daunting, flash fiction forces the prose writer to think like a poet. Writers of flash must pull away from our traditional narrative tendencies and focus on the implied, the unexplained, and even the mysterious. We draw from the universal and the political, that which is largely known and commonly experienced. We simply do not have enough time to explain or elaborate; we must quickly establish a common ground and move on.

Quite often, the structure of a flash piece jars us out of our lengthy and exhaustively descriptive prose and into a realm where music, rhythm, and wordplay convey our shared human experience. This form forces us to be nitpicky with our prose, and requires us to eliminate all the unnecessary (adjectives, adverbs, prepositions, etc.) and some of the necessary (plot, character, description, dialogue). Through its constraints, we are given a freedom that novelists and short-story writers can only dream of. We are not bogged down by a narrative or the traditional elements of fiction. We are free to write openly about those large subjects that most truly convey the human experience.

—Shanna Yetman

mw

THE MIRACLE IS TO WALK THIS EARTH

Shanna Yetman

Her son's surgery is thursday. His face is uneven, bulgy on one side. From the back, he looks like he's swallowed a balloon. His cyst, tumor, lipoma protrudes from the left side of his neck—as though someone has knotted up this growth and tied it with string.

But today they are at the park. Her son gestures for her to push him on the swings.

"Mama! Mama! Lift me up." He's managed to place himself halfway in the baby swing so it's easy for her to lift him into it. First, she puts down her book—a book written by a monk, with one of those single-word self-help titles like *fear, death, life, loss, gain, mindfulness.* She finds answers to her anxieties in Buddhism.

There is no fear in the present moment, she reminds herself.

She places her fingers on his back, pushes. She watches him rise and fall, rise and fall. He sings. She counts her breath, tries to match it with each movement of the swing.

Six in. *My heart is now at peace.*

Six out. She stops to push her breath out, to connect her body to her mind, anchoring herself to the present moment. No past. No future. Just now.

"Faster, Mama. Faster." He's three. When will he know? She feels guilty for not preparing him for the risks she consented to on his behalf. She feels guilty for giving him a body that needs surgery.

They hear the squawk of seagulls flying toward the lake. They watch a shower-like sprinkler go on and off, on and off every five minutes to the horror and joy of the children. Each time the sprinkler goes off, the water pours over the heads of those brave few and she and her son laugh. Each child shocked, surprised at the water's intensity.

"Do you want to go in? I brought your bathing suit."

"Just watch, Mama." He twists himself around to face her. "They don't know when it's coming." The sprinkler comes on and he laughs, claps his hands. "Swing more, Mama. Swing more."

She looks past her son to the choppy waters of Lake Michigan. She sees the individual waves, whitecaps wash over and over each other. Each one its own entity, coming up out of the water and then washing right back into it. For a while, she watches them come and go, come and go. She feels an incredible sadness every time a wave hits the shore or splashes against the pier.

No birth? No death? Her son's birth was such a happy memory. A blue-green day in early spring. She knows if she looks up, away from the waves, she will see the whole lake. Those waves are only water, after all. She remembers that first tug of her son's lips on her nipples, the let down of her first milk, and the end of breastfeeding. The pain that came with breasts stuffed rock-hard with milk no child would drink. She can't help but look at those waves, stare at them obsessively. They are small, nothing compared to what the ocean might produce, but they are enough for her. She watches the wind seduce the lake into one frothy wave after another. She thinks she sees one begin to rise way back and float forward. She hopes it will break past the pier, past the beach even, and closer to her—washing over her, maybe?

She wants it to last as long as it can and then rage to the end.

The 39th

New Millennium Fiction Award

Jackie Davis Martin

KNIFE

Jackie Davis Martin's most recent stories appear online in *Fractured West*, *Bluestem*, *On the Premises*, and *Thrice Fiction*, and in print anthologies: *Modern Shorts*, *Love on the Road*, and *Life is A Rollercoaster*. A memoir, *Surviving Susan*, was published in 2012.

She teaches at City College of San Francisco.

In my own writing life, I have been challenged by, and enjoyed taking, writing classes and both one-day and week-long workshops. I love being involved with other writers, receiving good criticism, learning new tools of the craft. I love being in the company of other writers. Beyond those peripheral gains—or below them, perhaps—is the day-to-day efforts of putting words to paper. Provocative writing prompts help a great deal. I believe in prompts to stir the imagination, stimulate the soul, uncover old longings. It helps me to write a little each day, particularly in the morning when my mind works in ways that surprise me. Afternoons are good for reflection, for editing and reshaping. I enjoy having a good writing partner and belonging to a committed writing group. As far as what I write, well, in my case I start with me—an image, a setting, a feeling, my immediate or distant past—and take off from there. Fiction can be quite liberating.

—Jackie Davis Martin

KNIFE

Jackie Davis Martin

T HAT SATURDAY EVENING, Lila and her husband Graham were at a dinner party for six—somewhat small-scale for their hostess Janelle—where they sat stiffly on antique Chinese chairs around Janelle's table and exclaimed over salad served on the asymmetrical plates she'd brought from Paris. The three couples were accustomed to one another and always on the alert for a new flourish at the table. Lila found comments on dining accoutrements tiresome and irrelevant, although she too joined in with compliments on the placemats from India, a centerpiece from Prague. Lila longed for something new to happen. Soon the dinner party conversation would switch to travel and become more tedious. These were her old friends! She tried to listen. Anthony, the host, was elaborating on why they'd chosen this condo complex (garage, gardens, privacy) and the garrulous Margaret kept interrupting to talk of her and Mike's recent find: a condo they'd move into when they returned from Berlin. It was easy for Lila to drift, to poke desultorily at the purple greens (odd description in itself) as she toyed with one of Janelle's exquisite butter knives.

"Ah," Anthony said. "Those belonged to Janelle's grand-mother. Aren't they pretty?"

The knives nudged Lila back to a time when she took risks. She remembered Innsbruck, she and Graham sitting at a sidewalk café. Had it really been twenty-five years ago? There had been a round wrought-iron table and slatted wood chairs, the two of them leaning over their thick tureens of coffee and sharing an apple strudel. "Mit Schlag!" they always added. They'd order only one so they could stop again and order another, the way they made love then, always the stop temporary, the pleasure keen but already anticipating the next indulgence, smug in the knowledge it would occur.

They'd been sitting at an Innsbruck café with mountains on all sides, snow-peaked even in summer, and, when Graham consulted his map, Lila slipped the scrolled knife they'd been served with the strudel into the pocket of her jacket. "Life doesn't get any better than this," he had observed.

She'd leaned across and whispered, "I stole the knife."

His eyes scanned the empty plate. "Where? Put it back."

"No," she said. "Anyway, I have others, too, but not as pretty."

"What! Christ, Lila."

"In the suitcase. This makes five, I think."

Graham thought the Austrian consuls would find out or something. Even then, Lila had recognized in him his attention to the right thing, waiting one's turn, not making waves, qualities that were in stark contrast to the man she had dated before him, who had asserted and bullied their way into the best rooms, the extra soaps and towels, the table with the window view.

On that same trip she'd helped herself to one more little knife—this time from a restaurant in a small town on their way to Salzburg—to round out her set. When they'd returned home, Lila didn't display her collection as she'd intended, as she might have done for Lucky—that was the former boyfriend's name, how odd she hadn't thought of it. Lucky. He was, too; he got away with things. She was wowed by and mistrusting of him. Lila didn't consider that Graham was unlucky—lack of luck didn't necessarily accompany a solid sense of fair play—just not as edgy. She had tucked her knives into a plastic baggie and stashed them at the rear of the utensil drawer, where, from time to time, she'd look at them, remembering her daring.

It was literally a knock at the door. The entrance of the stranger at Janelle's and Anthony's dinner party shifted Lila's resigned perspective. Janelle was clearing the salad plates, preparing for Anthony to serve his hunter's pork stew. Anthony had recently taken a cooking class. If you studied Janelle's face—always gracious—you could see her anxiety over the ordinariness of what her husband accomplished. To balance things out, she used designer pottery. The stew arrived in glazed bowls, each in the shape of a different flower, which they raved about and then, remembering the stew, commented on that, too.

But the knocking on the door was sudden and firm. Anthony said, "I'll get it," and pushed himself from his chair; Graham was forced to wrap up some comment which had gone on too long already about Obama's policies, and Lila felt a little sorry for him. She was more attuned, however, to the man who stepped into the room, bringing in with him gusts of fog and a scent of lilies from the gardens outside.

He was a short man, rather rotund, with a gray crew-cut, thickly soft, like bristles on a baby's brush. He wore a handsome gray raincoat over a plaid flannel shirt and corduroy trousers. He talked rapidly: hated to bother, had just moved in, couldn't get the damn garage door opener to work, car blocking sidewalk, squeezed through bushes, wife not here yet, sorry to bother—but?

"Come back!" Janelle called as Anthony retrieved keys and exited with the stranger. "Come back and join us for dessert."

He returned with a bottle of wine clutched by its neck. He said he'd had cases delivered, but no opener and forgot to get one, having been distracted by "an encounter in a bar where some guy—right out of Dostoevsky—clutched my shirt and wouldn't shut up." His name was Bill Barnes and he had just been hired at SF State as an exchange professor. Lila placed his age at mid-fifties, maybe. Not too many years younger than she was—but what a thought.

He dug with gusto into Janelle's strawberry galette and said he'd been living on flavored coffees and Big Macs as he crossed the country. Lila reached for one of the table's bottles in its earthenware holder to refill his glass. Bill Barnes glanced her way in a brief thanks and Lila's heart fluttered as though she were thirteen. The man's eyes were light under pronounced eyelids. It was his vitality—he was so different from them.

"You'll have to come over for coffee," Janelle was saying now. "Anthony and I are always here—except when we travel."

Lila feared that Margaret, who set down her fork, would jump in on cue at the word "travel," but she was on another course. She began a recitation of professors from SF State that she'd been aware of one way or another.

Lila wanted them to shut up.

"Decaf, anyone?" Janelle said. "Brandy?"

Bill Barnes apologized for crashing their party, but was easily persuaded to stay. He watched Anthony uncork a new bottle. "My own wine opener, a real beauty, was confiscated last year at the Houston airport," he said.

Anthony was sympathetic. "Goddam security stuff in override. All the time."

"My wife... sent a knife," Graham began. They all laughed.

"Graham writes poetry," Lila said, and felt mean, although it was true. Graham played around with four-syllable rhymes—"My mood/ Has changed with the food"—which sometimes amused her and other times made her want to scream. He once in awhile wrote a real poem, a good one, that didn't rhyme at all. Graham was launched, though, into the story of Lila's packing a paring knife that had been almost confiscated by security in its own box to send along with their luggage; the box had

arrived bobbing along on the conveyor belt at the baggage
claim. Graham was too slow with anecdotes, Lila thought,
although deliberation was one of the qualities she'd once
liked in him.

"That reminds me," she said, wanting to jolt them. "I stole
knives. Six of them, in Austria, years ago. They're in the
rear of the drawer."

"You did what?" Margaret said. She jutted her head
forward.

"She said she stole knives," Anthony said. "This sounds
good." Anthony was clearly getting drunk. His wife busied
herself with demitasses and tiny glasses with golden scrolls.

"'In the Rear of the Drawer,'" Bill Barnes announced.
"A good title. Are you a writer?"

"Yes. No." Lila thought of her own intense concentration
at the computer, her creation of several stories, three of
which had been published in online journals. She stared at
the man, at his fuzzy crop of hair: Bill, William. Surely—?
She'd read the stories of William Baker Barnes in *Harper's*,
in *The New Yorker*—she owned two paperback collections.
She'd admired his economy of presentation, the intensity
of situation and unusual characters. "My God," she said.
"You're William Baker Barnes!"

"He *said* Barnes," Anthony said.

Lila drained her brandy quickly and Bill—William—did
the same. He glanced her way and bobbed his head in a
sort of affirmation. She didn't want to make a fool of herself
gushing over him. Margaret, who clearly had never heard
of William Baker Barnes, told him that when she'd taught
high school several people had told her that she should
write. She smiled humbly at her disclosure.

"And you?" Bill Barnes asked Lila.

"Not like you. But—yes. I do write."

A hour and a few travel anecdotes later, Anthony gathered their coats and they all said goodbye in the vestibule. Lila thought that Bill Barnes smiled at her differently from the others, as though she were a kindred soul, but she considered maybe she just wanted to see that.

The next morning Lila spilled the pot of coffee she'd just made. It was more than a spill—it was a river of coffee that spread across countertop to floor. She'd used the last of her beans, and now she had to throw down towels, get on her knees, to mop up. Both Janelle and Margaret had "someone in" to do cleaning, and probably William Baker Barnes and his wife would, too.

The name gave her a pleasant and unpleasant start that—getting another towel—she forced herself to examine. She'd met a writer she truly admired, someone of talent beyond those in her writing group—although they'd all learned to be good critics—but it was Janelle who lived almost next door, and Janelle didn't care. Lila tried to remember what Barnes looked like—sort of like one of those inflatable punching dolls from her childhood, not roly-poly exactly, but solid, of a piece. It was the confidence he exuded: this is who I am; my talent enables me to be daring.

She needed caffeine.

Graham was just getting up as Lila pulled on last night's jacket, still draped over the balustrade. "Starbucks," she explained. "We're out of coffee."

"What?" The gray strands of his hair looked electrically charged. "You don't like Starbucks."

"Be right back."

At Starbucks, the paper fluttered to the floor when Lila pulled her hand out of her pocket. A woman behind her picked it up and handed it to her. It was a bank withdrawal slip with writing on it: "Call me. Stolen knives, stolen lives. Bill B." And his number. Lila dropped the free cup of coffee she'd got with the pound of beans and created the second mess that morning.

"I want you to read this story I've been working on," he said when she called. "It's about a knife—or letter opener, anyway."

"Me?" Sunday morning gathered itself where she sat, on a bench outside Walgreen's, cars half into the street waiting for their turn to enter the lot. Such an ordinary hubbub for her to be talking to the likes of William Baker Barnes! Maybe he had seen insight and intelligence in her.

"Is today a possibility?"

She told Graham she forgot about a baby shower for a woman in her department. "Who?" he asked, even though he was familiar with only three or four names. She told herself that this meeting was of no more consequence than such an event, although her heart was racing and she was vowing not to boast to her writing group. She'd take the meeting in stride. If she ran into Janelle or Anthony—what then? What would she say? She wouldn't have needed to sneak through bushes to invite William Baker Barnes to visit her classroom. It was all pretty nerve-wracking and—she had to admit—a thrill.

William Baker Barnes—she had to stop calling him three names in her head even though he didn't seem to be a "Bill" at all—was waiting at the end of the garden. As he admitted her through an iron gate, Lila glanced through thick tall shrubs to determine the orientation of the condo complex.

Bill smiled. "They'd be over that way. Your friends." He led her away from where he'd pointed, the shrubs so dense and fountains so loud that Lila was assured her presence was undetected. Besides, her focus was mostly on the hand, large and warm and slightly damp, that gripped her own.

She was struck by the clean lines and spaces of his unit. Janelle and Anthony's home was so overwrought with window dressings and furniture and rug upon rug that one didn't think in terms of rooms at all. Here what would become the living room was now empty except for a buttress of wine boxes at one end. An opened bottle, a cheap corkscrew, and a plastic goblet sat on the kitchen counter next to crumpled paper coffee cups.

"I started without you," he said. "But I'm prepared to entertain." He shook loose another goblet from a large bag and poured two glasses.

A card table and one folding chair took up the dining area; there was a laptop, a small printer and stack of papers and files. Her heart pounded: William Baker Barnes at work.

He assessed her assessment. "Yeah, it's great in a way. Wait'll Francie gets here, though. The space will close in."

The name took Lila aback; suddenly she felt like the other woman, a position she'd never had or considered. He led her through a second room, totally empty, past a bathroom where she noted soggy towels on the floor, reminiscent of her own kitchen that morning, to a large room with an unmade futon in its center. Scattered clothes and suitcases surrounded the futon, as though it were a floating island. She paused in the doorway. "This unit seems so different from Anthony's and Janelle's."

"'Anthony and Janelle,'" he said. "Who can go on saying those awkward names? If you wrote about them, you'd have to call them something else."

"Why would I write about them?"

He'd entered the bedroom and was setting the glasses carefully on a box of wine that was functioning as a nightstand;

a cheap goose-neck lamp leaned inquiringly next to keys and small change. He flopped onto the futon, patting the space next to him. The sheets were navy blue and new, their plastic zipper case flung in a corner. Lila stood in the doorway wondering what to do, and he laughed at her wavering. "I'm offering you the only available seating," he said.

She set her handbag on the floor, folded her jacket on top of it, and crawled on all fours, joining him. She hadn't been this close to anyone but Graham in twenty-six years.

"What do you write about?" he said conversationally, as though he really was curious. At the same time he was reaching under a heap of clothes to produce a cluster of printed pages. "Ah, I knew it was here. I was re-reading it last night prior to sending it to my agent."

Of course he would have an agent; she just sent out things at random. At a summer conference, a minor writer had told her her writing resembled Joyce Carol Oates's; he'd urged her to try for an agent, but she'd felt shy about it. Now Lila admitted that comment to Bill and he raised his eyebrows. "Do you make things up?" he said. "Or do you use experiences like the stolen knives?"

She kept glancing at the story, *his*, right there.

"How many knives are there?"

He was interested; she could answer. "Altogether? Hmm—eight. Six from traveling with Graham, two from Lucky—a guy I dated before Graham."

"All stolen?"

"Yes." She shrugged, feeling a little pride at the minor filching that seemed to attract him.

He asked if she'd be tempted to write about him, and when she demurred—why would she do that—he insisted.

"You?" She wanted to impress, yet he liked honesty.

"A writer of fifty. Fifty-five? Hair like a grey baby-chick, a sort of permanent smirk. I'd give you glasses."

He laughed. "Wires? Tortoise?"

"I don't know! I'd have to know you better."

"I can do you, easily." He guessed her age at fifty or so, too, and she didn't add the extra years. A good body, he said, and charming bangs. He touched her hair. "A Matron-Femme Fatale-Little Girl."

Lila shivered. She sipped her wine. Had she any lipstick on at all? Just as she thought that, William Baker Barnes leaned forward and kissed her, a brief and warm press of the lips. "With beautiful lips," he said. "Perfect lips." She was wide-eyed; it was a surprise, a transgression. And yet—she had to admit—such an enormous compliment to be desired. She tried not to say to herself: *by a famous writer.*

He smiled gently and leaned on his elbow, relaxing, as though they'd known each other in one way a long time and he was now contemplating another. "What do you do? Do you have lovers?"

"Have?" She set down her glass and picked up his story, amazed more by the casual presumption of the question than she'd been at the indiscretion they'd both committed. "You mean present tense. No." The words on his papers ran together.

"Go ahead," he said. "Read." He cued her in with a little butt of his head.

"Do you really want my comments? What do you want?" She twisted to sit up, positioning herself like a child, legs jutting out. She had to look at him over her shoulder.

He sat up, too. It was an odd arrangement, as though they were on a beach blanket, basking without sun, without an ocean. Her dark blue jeans ended in black boots;

his corduroy legs ended in black socks with the gold stitching on the toes, the same socks her husband wore.

"What do I want." He said it as though it was a large concept, one he'd been deliberating for a while. "Fame. Love. Money."

She wondered whether he was making fun of her. "You have those, don't you?"

"Shit," he said. "In maybe some communities. Did your friends know who I was? Would I be accepting another position involving all this moving?" He planted his feet on the floor and heaved himself up with some effort. She felt dismissed. It was her own fault; she'd brought herself here, knowing nothing of him but his name. What did *she* want?

"Relax," he said, padding across the room. "I'm getting refills. Read."

Lila returned to the story, looking for the letter-opener he'd mentioned. There was one. The girl, a child, stabbed her brother with it, pretending a game, and severed an artery. Lila held her breath in dismay—the audacity of stabbing a child on paper.

"How do you do this?" she asked after three pages. "How do you plunge right in and create chaos? Heartbreak?" Mostly she'd been told she skirted around the issue in her work instead of facing it head-on.

He set the bottle
carefully on the
carton and fell onto the
flat bed in a lump. "That's just
it," he said. "I plunge."

He wrapped his arms around her
and pulled her down.

He kissed her again, this time with a passion that stirred
and confused her. His body was solid against hers, his
mouth solid, too. He released her and held her, her head
cradled on his shoulder. "You feel good," he said. "Don't
you think this all feels good?"

She hadn't protested. She had just allowed it to
happen, and he was right: it did feel good. She stared
beyond his chest to the blank walls, the bare hallway
with its staircase, the space. It was an unfurnished
world of no past or present. So she told herself.
Even so, after two more kisses she said she really
had to get home, and he said take the story with
you, what about Thursday?

Early Thursday evening Bill turned toward her
on his bar stool, reminding Lila of years spent
before she married Graham, of scenes in the
early eighties, her sitting on bar stools swiveling
toward a stranger that she hoped would turn into
someone steady, someone she could stop going
to bars to have to meet. "So, what did you think?
The story."

She didn't know whether the thrill of William
Baker Barnes asking her opinion outweighed the
conspicuousness of where they were. She'd agreed
on this bar because it was in a part of the city she
never frequented; now, however, she felt uneasy.

Prompted by Bill's text messages and the duration of his temporary bachelordom, she'd told Graham she'd signed up for a new writing course for the next four Thursday evenings, so she'd already committed herself to this one. Then Francie (Francie! she sounded cute, and young) would arrive, and Lila would pretend Bill Barnes hadn't happened in this particular way.

"So tell me." He leaned an elbow across the bar, propping his head to look at her.

"I didn't believe the child would stab her brother."

"Okay," he said. She expected him to say "Why not?" or "Kids can be cruel." Was he dismissing her already? Or actually listening?

"It's too sudden. Maybe she has a mean streak—whatever that is—planted earlier. Maybe she considers grilling bugs with a magnifying glass, maybe she does."

"Nice detail, that. Did you?"

"Actually, yes. But I didn't stab my brother. I didn't have a brother."

"I did," he said. "I used a popsicle stick, but it broke and the spike tore his skin."

"Like the letter opener."

"Like a knife," he said. He squinted, as though focusing on something in his head, silent for a moment. "So—okay, I'll work in some other detail. Let's talk about your knives. Your motives."

She told him she wanted to hold onto something.

"What?"

"What I thought was elusive. Something rare that...satisfied."

"No guilt? Remorse?"

She shook her head. "No."

He smiled. "Let's go to my place," he said. "We have lots to talk about."

How could she possibly refuse a writing idol? She told herself she would learn from a master. He held the door for her: "It will be our first *craft* session," he said.

He liked undressing her slowly, which she allowed, no longer hiding behind her going-on-sixty sense of herself. She had some varicose veins and breasts that sagged a little without their bra, but here on the mattress, without the pressures of gravity, she could hold her own. Besides, he didn't seem to see flaws. His lovemaking was warm and gentle and, if she admitted the truth, a teeny-bit boring with its lack of urgency.

He said he'd married young, in college, and had strayed only three times since then, although that seemed hard to believe. She pried for experiences prior to the marriage, only to keep his on a keel even with her own, but he had been focused on writing even then, a misfit, he described himself as, in a situation that prohibited much sexual exploration.

He saw his present condo with its echoing rooms as a teenager would a house emptied by vacationing parents. After two visits, Lila too lost all sense that her friends lived across the thick garden, beyond one of the babbling fountains.

She didn't lose the sense of Graham sitting at home. He was a fair man and much better in bed than Bill Barnes. Barnes had a fine public sense of himself, forceful and convincing, but in bed he was another matter—tentative and too deliberate, as though he'd read a manual. Graham was gentle and thorough, so her betrayal here with Bill was deep. She couldn't shake the way things should be done, had been done for twenty-six years, and get into what was seemingly a performance on Bill's part, which left her satisfied, eventually, it was true, but not exactly dying to go through the entire thing all over again.

Still, she loved telling herself that William Baker Barnes was her lover; it was thrilling—the furtive meetings, his intrigue with her, her novelty of him. And she did probe him about form and voice, about revision tactics: How did he figure out what to cut? He'd been amused at that question: "Cut? A bit obsessed with the image, aren't you?" But he'd answered seriously; one simply determined what was not essential to the situation, not needed, then got rid of it.

He pressed her to tell him of her affairs. When she said none, he said never, not before marriage? Oh, well, that, she said. "That," he'd said. "Tell me." He seemed to admire her as a woman of experience, and she felt exhilarated with the position he'd assigned her; he was a mere writer—she was a woman who had lived.

"There was a game," she said, "many years ago—when I was single for a while." They knew this phrase to mean between marriages, although he didn't ask which ones. "It was all a contrivance—this social event—where we tried to get to know someone, scope someone out. *What makes you happy?* That was the game. It was a drill; we'd keep asking the question of a partner—a stranger—and he—or she—had to keep answering, keep coming up with new answers."

Bill Barnes's eyes scrunched with mirth. At such times he looked boyish and Lila wanted to hug him. "That's great. And you, for instance, answered…?"

"Probably the usual—books, sky, ice cream—I don't remember. But I know the answer to the other question now." She was sitting as he was, knees pulled up, arms around them. "About the knives. I wanted to steal my own happiness."

They were on his futon and he reached around her to refill the empty glasses that had been sitting on the box. "Do I make you happy?"

She tried to assess what he might have in mind: his writing, his status in her eyes? Maybe he was just speaking of sex, though. "Yes," she said. She didn't ask back, not wanting him to have to fudge an answer, too.

On the last Thursday of September, Barnes had champagne for the two of them; the days were beginning to darken early. On Saturday his furniture would arrive, as would Francie, filling in the role Lila had temporarily usurped. Francie called daily, once even in Lila's presence. Bill had spoken to Francie with the mouth that had just been on Lila's. She wondered whether he felt guilty, but his wink to her told her the conspiracy was private and mutual.

"Won't you be upset?" he asked that last evening, cradling her, the way he did after.

"We've known all along," she said. "Will you?"

"It doesn't have to end," he said. "Would you be upset if it ended? It doesn't have to."

"I don't see how it can go on." Life would be guilt-free, she considered with a small relief, guilt-free and ordinary. She wished for a moment that she still smoked; a cigarette seemed a good idea right now.

"Will you take anything?" he said. He gestured, as though offering the apartment.

"Take?" She considered she'd already taken something that wasn't hers. "You mean as in steal?"

His lips turned up—a smile, or a smirk. "Well, it's been our space and it'll be taken from us." He said Francie loved to entertain; she'd want to meet the people he worked with. And Janelle and Anthony had been kind. They could all get together, like the night he met her. "And your husband, too—what's his name—the poet?"

Lila reached for her jeans. "I've got to be going."

He watched her dress and checked his cell phone. "It's

almost ten o'clock," he said. "Your 'class' is over." She was in his bathroom, combing her hair; he came to stand behind her, lifted her hair and kissed her neck. "Did you learn anything—in class?"

She spoke to the mirror. "I did, yes. I learned to face the words, that words can pierce."

He loosened his arms. "You're talking about writing."

"It was a writing class," she said, now moving into his writing room where her jacket hung over the sole chair. "And you? You took the class, too." She longed to look at what he was working on; she wondered if she'd had any effect.

"Actually, I did learn something." She was grateful for the word *actually*; it made it easier to walk away from him. "I learned—again—that people can be...forthcoming."

It was late November—two months later—that Lila saw the story. She discovered it in *The Atlantic*, and she looked up Bill's schedule online to find his office phone, not his cell where they often left innocuous messages, and rang him directly. He feigned delight at first, at hearing from her at work, but immediately grew defensive at her attack. He had merely borrowed a bit of a situation, he said.

"Situation? You made it your story." The phone was a mistake. She had no upper ground with a flat plastic device wedged next to her ear. She saw William Baker Barnes sitting at a desk, his feet perhaps propped on an open drawer, the power to say whatever he wanted, or to say nothing at all.

He asked her whether she'd written the story, too, another version, and when she said no, he questioned her alarm. "We're writers," he said. "Borrowing is what we writers do."

"But you stole," she said.

"Stole," he said. "That's your word, Lila."

He added that already he'd been contacted by one of the editors of *Best Short Stories of The Year,* who'd read it ahead of publication.

She pressed "Cancel" without saying goodbye.

Through tears of fury she reopened *The Atlantic* and read, in one of the formats she had revered for years, "Knife," by William Baker Barnes. In the story he called her character "Lilian." An artist of around sixty, pretty but aging, Lilian seeks out the attentions of a talented young photographer, Bjorn, whom she falls in love with. She is so much in love with him that she senselessly steals knives from their steak dinners. When her husband Garrett discovers the knives, her affair is revealed. Bjorn has an enormously successful exhibition, where he stands proudly with his wife Fawn and pretends not to know Lilian. One is left with the suggestion that Lilian returns to kill herself with one of the stolen knives.

Lila folded the magazine closed and sat there until darkness began to descend and Graham returned from the store. He asked what was wrong. She couldn't say "Nothing," so she said an article on death had affected her. He nodded and touched her shoulder briefly as he left the room, and she felt worse at the simple trust he had endowed her with.

"Lila?" Graham called from the kitchen. "Honey? Do you want some cheese and crackers? I just got this aged Gouda."

She heard the fridge open and shush closed, the sound of the cheeseboard being slammed onto the counter. Possibly no one would recognize the likeness of the story's initials. Or, how many in her social set would read the story? Would they associate her at all, even with the knives? And—here was an important point—Bill had actually asked whether she'd written it too, suggesting she could. She at least had that from the affair: the fact that he respected her writing and saw her as competition, in a way. She considered that maybe she would write something about a vain writer who made use of a woman who—

A kitchen drawer banged up and down being jimmied, and Graham cursed then cried out at the crash. When Lila rushed in, Graham, a little stunned, was getting slowly to his knees amid the overturned drawer and its spilled contents. He picked up spatulas and ladles, as well as the plastic bag of little stolen knives. On his knees, he handed the bag to Lila, smiling with his usual kindness, shrugging away sins of the past. She took the utensils he held out to her and shoved them into the drawer, noisily righting it, slamming it closed, and then offered Graham her arm for him to stand.

The 40th

New Millennium Fiction Award

Nina Varela

THE THINGS WE DID IN TEXAS

Nina Varela is a nationally awarded writer of screenplays and short fiction. She majors in Writing for Screen & Television BFA ('17) at the University of Southern California School of Cinematic Arts. Besides writing, Nina enjoys baking, Netflix, and sweater weather.

She can be reached at *www.ninavarela.com.*

*A*S A QUEER WOMAN — PARTICULARLY *one poised to enter the male-dominated Hollywood film industry upon graduation — it is important to me to write stories about women, LGBT+ people, neuroatypical people, and people of color. There is no greater feeling than reading a book or watching a TV show and identifying so strongly with one of the characters, relating to their fears and desires, understanding their perspective so completely, that you learn something new about yourself. I know that feeling, and I crave that feeling, and I also know how frustrating it is to search for a relatable character in a piece of media and find none. So I always want to write those underrepresented characters, to give them a voice and a story.*

With "The Things We Did in Texas," I attempted to take a classically male (white, heterosexual) narrative, set in the American Old West, and retell it with decidedly un-classic characters. Storytelling is, above all else, a way to communicate this: You are not alone. That's my goal when I write. I hope I have succeeded.

—Nina Varela

THE THINGS WE DID IN TEXAS

Nina Varela

I PICK HIM BECAUSE HE looks like he could walk away from all of this no problem, just up and run, and I like that in a person. All bones, too—gaunt face, jaw like a knife blade, collarbones thrusting up through the skin. I got a soft spot for bones, always did. So I watch him for days, propped up in the darkest corner of the bar, hiding my face behind my hair. I ask around town, prod the stubborn bartender until he talks. They all say this man, this skinny man with the silver flask and the deck of cards, is the best guide around. Knows Texas like a bird knows the wind.

He's sitting by the batwing doors today, slats of late afternoon sunlight falling across his hands, the rest in shadow. I toss back the rest of my whiskey, a line of heat from throat to belly, and hop off my barstool. There's only seven creatures in here total: me, him, the bartender, two old men smoking in a gloomy corner, a painted lady, and an ancient dog. It's not late enough for the evening crowd, not early enough for the whiskey-breathers, the drunks who spent the night.

He can definitely hear me coming toward him, but he don't look up until I'm standing right over his table, stripes of sunlight turning my dress into a jailbird's costume. Then he raises his head and looks me dead-on, his eyes darker than a moonless sky. I gesture at the cards. "You playin' Patience?"

He's silent for a moment, just looking at me, and then his mouth twists into something like a smile. "Nah. Only card game I ever learned is War."

"Well goddamn if you ain't the worst Texan I ever heard of," I say, "and I ain't even heard of you."

"You gonna sit?"

I sit. The chair scrapes against the wooden floor, and the painted lady glances over lazily. Nobody else bats an eye. I pull the deck of cards toward me, shuffling quickly and stacking them up even. "You gotta at least learn how to play Patience."

He watches me quietly, eyes in shadow. The bars of sunlight slide across the table. Twilight falls fast in this town, the sun sinking to its knees as if shot.

"Patience," I say, dealing out the seven columns of cards to face him. "French call it Solitaire. All you wanna do is make four piles, king at the top, ace at the bottom. Black, red, black, red."

"What do I get when I win?" he asks, turning a card over. His eyes flick over my face.

"A job."

"Well, now," he says, flipping over the king of spades, "that's interesting."

When the world ended I was laughing wildly, stumbling down the icy street, drunk out of my mind. Jessamine's arm was draped across my shoulders, her skin cold and damp with New England fog, smelling like smoke, booze, burnt sugar beneath it all. She was telling some story she'd told a hundred times before, her breath rushing hot against my neck. The fog dusted my hair, my eyelashes, glittering on my skirts like tiny stars. My ears still rang from the noise of the barflies hollering, singing, women shrieking and whooping with laughter, all propriety forgotten. But the streets in this part of Boston were hushed, the windows dark, the storefronts cracked and yellowed like old teeth.

Jessamine and I were the loudest around. We always were. Men saw us, the pretty girls with the wide, pretty mouths, and got all hushed.

"Flora," Jessamine said, tongue thick, words slow as molasses, "Flor, I just thought of the funniest thing," and I said, "What's that?" and she started to say something but pulled up short. Her mouth snapped shut with a click.

"What's the funniest thing, Jessie, tell me," I said, patting her face. We were twenty years old and looked like we'd been dipped in starlight. When the world ended.

"**N**ame's Thatch," he tells me, slapping a red ace onto the third pile. Either he lied about not knowing how to play Patience, or he just picks things up quickly.

"Flora," I say.

"Flora," he repeats. "Well, Miss Flora, you gonna tell me about that job?"

I raise an eyebrow. "What do you think, Mister Thatch?"

"I think you're clever," he says quietly, focused on the cards. "Cleverer than me. I think you been on your own for a while, which is why you was drinkin' straight whiskey.

And I think you know exactly what you want from me. So, Miss Flora." He looks at me. "Where do you wanna go?"

I lean forward on my elbows, my hair brushing the table. He keeps his eyes above my chin, doesn't steal a glance at the curving neckline of my dress. I appreciate him for it. We sit there in silence, haloed in gold by the setting sun, until he's got four neat piles of cards. The dog sits up, stretches, scratches its fleas. Thatch takes a pull from his flask.

"I need a horse," I tell him.

"I can get you a horse. Where do you wanna go?"

I shift in my chair, swallowing hard. It feels like I got something buried in my chest, something sharp and hot. "Well," I say, "problem is I been lots of places, but I only *really* know West Texas."

"Right," he says. "So where do you wanna go?"

"Coast." I take a deep breath. "All the way across the state. I got eighty dollars. All yours."

Thatch raises his eyebrows, and I know what he's thinking—girl like me shouldn't have that kind of money. He's wondering who I robbed, who my daddy is, how many times I whored. But he don't ask. He just says, "You got bags?"

"Just the one," I tell him, and we stand up together and push through the batwing doors, out onto the empty street, silhouetted against the purple dusk.

We went to Boston because she wanted to see snow, and I wanted to see her see snow.

When you grow up in the desert of Texas, you gotta be careful. There's something about the bigness—the pale dirt, the endless cornflower sky, the dry brush and dust storms and the blistering sun—that catches hold of you. Licks across your skin, swallows you and all your broken pieces like a snake swallowing an egg. If you ain't careful, you'll get stuck. The desert will never let you out alive. So Jessamine wanted to see snow.

We left in November, took the railroad from the bone-dry flats to the wet winter of New Orleans, from New Orleans to Virginia, and from Virginia to steely New York, where the men dressed in sack suits and black bowlers. We stayed a few nights in each new city, drinking the men under the table in a dozen different bars, Jessie slipping her hand into their pockets while I ran my fingers through my hair and bit my bottom lip. We ate beignets in New Orleans, powdered sugar clinging to our chins. Biscuits and gravy in South Carolina, where a woman with silver hair and a moon-shaped face loaded our plates over and over again with fat strips of bacon. In New York, we ate German sausages smothered in onions, our tongues tasting of charcoal and sweet smoke. The ice turned gray beneath our boots. We got on another train.

In Boston, Jessie and I laid on a thin mattress in the spare room above a bakery, drank thick black coffee and shared a bag of saltwater taffies. Our back teeth stuck together when we chewed. We stayed up until dawn two nights in a row, and I remember how the watery sunlight fell across the floorboards, the air so cold it hurt to breathe. We mixed our coffee with Southern bourbon, and Jessie stumbled to her feet, wrapped in a blanket, her smile slow and sticky. When she leaned against the icy windowpane, it looked like she was leaning against a slab of that white winter sky.

I squinted up at her. "Baker says it's gonna snow again tomorrow. Says his leg aches and that's how he knows." I felt straw poking me through the mattress but was too lazy to move. The room kept tilting, balancing itself out like a set of scales.

Jessie slumped back a little bit. I watched her dark hair, the pale line of her throat. She said, "We could stay."

"We don't belong up here," I mumbled. "Ain't Texas."

"Texas got nothin' for me anymore."

I looked up at that. Jessie's mama died that past summer, just up and died, and that was about when Jessie started chasing snow. "Stay," I said, testing the shape of it, the weight.

"Stay," said Jessie. She smiled so big that I had to close my eyes and hang on to that damn straw mattress for dear life, because if I looked at her for one second longer I'd fly apart.

Six days into our three-week ride, somewhere in the western half of Edwards Plateau, Thatch and me stare into the glowing coals of our campfire. We lay on worn blankets, listening to the singing crickets, the wind rustling the long prairie grass, the crackling, snapping fire. Thatch's horses make their quiet horse noises, tails flicking. The moon hangs big and heavy in the black sky, a ripe fruit ready to fall.

Thatch hums quietly and rolls over, facing out across the dark swells of grassland.

I hug my bag tight to my chest.

He hasn't asked me why. I think somehow he knows.

Jessie and me were thirteen the first time it happened. We were sitting in the shade behind her house, our backs against the slats of gray wood, skirts pooled around us in the dirt.

It was the tail end of a Texas summer, the kind nobody escaped without burnt, peeling skin. My mama worked at Cotrell's in town for the months when my daddy and Jessie's daddy were away with the cows. Jessie's mama was already sick. That whole long, dry summer, Jessie and me just had each other. We played hide-and-seek in a land where scrub brush was the tallest thing around. We stuck our skinny arms through the gaps in fences, trying to make the horses eat parched grass from our palms. It stormed one day in late July, the sky cracking open from the weight of it, and we stripped down to our white underclothes and dirty bare feet, tilting our heads all the way back to taste the warm rain. Jessie reached out for my hand, muddy water snaking down her arm. I remember the slick mud between our fingers.

We were thirteen. It was August. Desert dust on our skirts, our hair, our holey shoes. You can't wash away that kind of dust. Even if you get out of Texas, it rides along in your lungs.

Jessie said, "Gimme your hand." I didn't question it. Just held my hand out. She said, "Close your eyes."

I closed my eyes. Something small dropped into my palm, and my eyes fluttered open to Jessie's toothy grin, her whole face crinkling up like wax paper. She had another piece of candy in her fingers, a twist of sticky brown horehound coated in white sugar.

She looked kinda surprised when I beamed at her. I didn't smile much, not even as a kid. Jessie was the bright one, the one who laughed at every joke, who cried when her daddy shot a cow. She'd always steal one of its bones once they'd sold off the meat, and we'd bury the bone under a prickly pear. Make a little cross out of rocks. We laid every one of those cows to rest, Jessie whispering a prayer over a small white bone, her eyelashes sticking with tears.

I dropped the candy on my tongue, the sweetness sizzling through my whole body, the best thing I'd tasted in months, all thick and heady. The two of us sat there until the last bit of sugar melted away. I drew in the dirt with my finger: a lopsided moon, some scattered X-mark stars.

When I looked up, Jessie was watching me. She had these big dark eyes, the same color as her curling hair. My eyes were the gray of old cloth.

"Thanks for the candy," I said. She didn't look away. "Well, what d'ya want from me?"

She shifted forward, bracing herself on the side of the house, and pressed her mouth to mine. I closed my eyes, out of instinct and vague memories from the one boy I'd kissed, so I just felt the dry softness of her lips, her fingers brushing the edge of my jaw. It only lasted a couple moments before she pulled away and we stared at each other, eyes wide.

That was the first time. And if there is one single thing I could be remembered for, one single thing I could put down in the history books, it's that Jessamine Lloyd tasted like dust and horehound candy and August heat. There are so many things I know, but I will never know anything more important than that.

On the eighth day, Thatch says he's got something to show me, only a few miles out of our way.

I say it's all right. We're in no hurry. We ride south all afternoon, keeping at a slow trot. The horses whicker at each other, big nostrils flaring, and there's a Godsent breeze against my sweaty skin. I never seen this much of Texas before—you only get so much from the windows of a train. I never seen this much green grass, bowing and stirring with the wind, or these many hills dotted with short, stubby trees.

Thatch rides in front, leading me up a small hill. He pulls at the reigns and turns to face me, his skinny self blocking out half of the setting sun, black gambler hat casting his face in even darker shadow. He smiles at me, cheekbones jutting out above the beginnings of a beard.

"I'm gettin' eighty dollars, right?" he says. "Well, this here's worth every penny of it."

I start to ask, but he just turns away again and disappears over the hill's crest. I dig my heels into my horse's side and we leap forward, my spine jolting with the force of it, following Thatch over the hill and toward the valley below.

When I see what he wanted to show me, I almost drop the reins.

At first I think the whole valley is purple, but that can't be right. I blink sweat out of my eyes and look again, and I know my jaw drops, but I can't help it. Millions of bluebonnets blanket the valley, stretching in all directions, every single one the rich purple-blue of summer twilight. The clusters of tiny buds sway like silent bells on their long green stems, dipping toward the dirt under the weight of bobbing honeybees. I breathe in deep, filling myself with the smell of them. Like the fresh soap from Cotrell's and like spring rain, light and sweet.

Thatch pulls his horse up beside mine. "You ever seen these before?"

"A few times," I say. My voice comes out raw. "Never this many, never like this."

He shrugs. "Figured with your name bein' Flora, you'd wanna see 'em."

"Well—thank you," I say quietly. "They're real pretty."

He nods, studying my face for a long moment, then kicks his horse and trots ahead of me, leaving a path of crushed flowers in his wake. I bow my head, trying to will away the hot burn behind my eyes.

I stopped school when I turned fifteen, but I'm smart. Always been smart. I know people turn to God when they can't explain things, when they're looking at destruction or creation and got no idea how it came to be. We talk to God most when we're holding another person, dead or just born or shuddering into our hands at night, and I know it's because that's a strange and terrifying and beautiful thing, the life and breath and loss of us, and nobody got any explanation for it, for everything we're made of and everything we become. I got no explanation either. But there are some things that bring me just to the edge of understanding, and the sight of these Texas bluebonnets, spreading over acres of land beneath the soft pink sky—well, that comes pretty damn close.

Thatch and me ride southeast through the rippling purple waves, and I think, *Someday I'll bury a cow bone here. I swear.*

We stayed in Boston. Of course we did—Jessie asked for it, and I was so gone on her. Nobody else could've understood it, how gone on her I was, ever since we were thirteen, maybe before. I didn't ever make a habit of running my mouth. Wasn't very friendly in general, actually. I mostly relied on Jessie to do the friendly for me. She'd sweet-talk anyone—men in bars, old women in general stores, strangers with spare rooms. I'd just stand there and look as pretty as I could, smiling big and dumb until my cheeks hurt. It worked every time. In Boston, we told everyone we were sisters. We didn't look much alike at all, but that was the power of Jessie.

It snowed all winter, December tumbling quickly into March, until I thought the whole sky might as well fall down on our heads. We worked at the bakery, living on leftover bread. The baker's wife gave us their dead daughter's old clothes, so we slogged through the snow-choked streets wrapped in the heat of a ghost, bought bacon fat and coffee and jugs of hard cider. At night we dipped chunks of bread into the pale brown fat, passing the cider back and forth until our bellies burned and laughter came easily.

One night, Jessie grabbed my hand and pulled me to the window. She breathed a warm circle onto the icy glass and widened it with her palm. We peeked out at the dark street, fingers still curled together. I remember the falling snow. Men stumbling home from bars. A lost scarf, a fingernail moon.

Jessie grinned into my neck. "Let's learn all the stars. All the"—she tripped over the word, just on the drunk side of tipsy—"con-stell-*a*-tions."

"How'd we go about doin' that?" I asked, tipping my head sideways, her hair brushing my cheek.

"I'm sure somebody in this city's got a book," she said. "A map. Somethin'. But imagine that, Flor. Imagine bein' anywhere in the world, and you look up, and you know exactly where you are."

"Anywhere in the world!" I laughed. "Where you gonna drag me next?"

"Well," she said. "We could sneak on a boat. I always wanted to see the ocean."

"Jess—," I started, but she cut me off, saying, "*Flora*," and nobody said my name like Jessie did. Like it really meant something, like it was maybe a bit more important than all the words around it. I looked at her then, and she was half silhouette, moonlight playing across her face. Gripping my hand so tight. Her lips quirked up in a sloppy smile.

We went to bed after that. When we were finished and Jessie collapsed to sleep, I stared at the wood rafters, drifting through my own head.

I remember wanting, that night, to tell Jessie we were different. If she was the moon, warm and round and glowing, then I was a falling star. I was a wild creature, something rough and fast, with hard edges and bruises and oftentimes a bloody lip. I was built messy, from whiskey and iron and the baked rocks of Texas, but thank God, I was also built from her. Softened by her, like a rock in a river. And still I was so selfish. And still I loved so crookedly: I wanted to swallow her whole, live inside of her, until there was no space left between us, until our hearts fit together and our breaths came fast.

But I couldn't. So instead I curled around her, the blankets gritty with that inescapable dust we'd carried all the way here, and I whispered those things into the darkness, quietly taking apart my ugly insides and placing each piece on the mattress, one by one, between me and the sleeping, breathing shape of her, me and the river, me and the collection of ghosts, the swell of bare skin, the seed stretching upward, searching for warmth in the white New England sky.

I wanted so hard to be her sunlight.

One week's ride from the East Texas coast and Thatch asks, "So who is it?"

I stare at my horse's twitching ears, pretending like I don't know what he's talking about. He raises his eyebrows at me and says, "I know why you hired me. Who is it?"

"None a your business," I say smoothly.

"It is my business," he says. "I'm takin' you all the way 'cross this Godforsaken state, so it's most certainly my business. If you didn't want it to be my business, you woulda took a train."

"No trains," I tell him without thinking. "On horse or on foot, but no trains."

"Why's that?" He doesn't look back at me. We're making a steady pace through brush country, with its red dirt and rough bushes, and there are enough cactuses that he can't glance away from the path. But I can feel his question hanging in the air like a mosquito, buzzing around my head.

I swallow hard and say, "Rode the trains with her. All the way up North, then back down here alone. So—never again."

"Why the coast?" Thatch asks.

"I don't wanna talk about it."

"I'm just thinkin'," he says loftily, skirting his horse around a prickly pear blooming with orange flowers, "it seems like an awful lotta trouble. I don't got a problem with it. I'm just wonderin' why."

"She always wanted to see the ocean." I take a deep, shaking breath, my voice barely loud enough for him to hear. "Snow and the ocean, and we saw snow. We were in Boston, you know, we coulda done it easy, but—it was so cold, we could barely leave our room, and we said we'd go in summer, but then—," I break off, digging my fingernails into the skin of my wrist. Hard enough that it leaves little red crescents behind.

Thatch don't reply for a long time, and I think it's done with. I close my eyes and trust my horse to follow Thatch's, just telling myself to breathe in and out, nice and steady.

Then he says, "Just an awful lotta work for someone who don't know it."

"Because that's what you *do*," I snap, suddenly wanting to lash out, kick him between the legs, make him cry and bleed. I want to scream at him: *Because that's what you do, don't you know that? You come back home, and you sleep in your old bed, and you learn the goddamn constellations 'cause that's what she wanted. You never go back North, not ever. You fix your own meals and eat them alone and go to sleep drunk and early, and your bed is so cold without her even at the height of Texas summer, and in the morning you still reach over to her side before you open your eyes, before you remember that she ain't curled up there anymore, never will be again, and—and—*

And you bury the dead for the rest of your life.

"It's somethin' I gotta get done," I say.

"As if it'll make any sense outta this mess," Thatch says, gesturing around us at the scrub brush and the horses and the clear blue sky, like it's more than what it is, like there's something broken and rotting beneath the surface. I realize he knows exactly what I mean. I was right, he's known the whole time. And I wonder who he's lost.

"I just gotta bring her to the ocean," I tell him, because I can't tell him anything else. "And I gotta do it the hard way."

He nods once, and I know he won't talk about it again.

She found me hollering beneath the noontime sun, my hair wild and dirty, blood dripping into my mouth from my busted nose. The boys were a hundred yards away and running fast, kicking up little clouds of dust, and I'm still proud to say they looked worse off than I did.

"Flora!" Jessamine yelled, and I swear for a second I thought she was her mama, even though we were sixteen and Jessie's mama hadn't gotten out of bed for a year. "What in the hell d'you think you're doin'?"

"They *started it*," I yelled right back. She ran up beside me and grabbed my shoulder, her other hand cupping my face. Her eyes darted across the blood and bruises, the mess I'd made of me. I tried to wrench away from her. "Jessie, they were—you didn't hear the kinda things they were sayin'!"

"All right, come on," she said, and dragged me off the dirt street into the tiny, shadowed alley between the old bank and Cotrell's. She pressed me back against one wall and fixed me with the hardest glare I'd ever seen. "Which one a them hit you?"

I didn't answer.

"Which one, Flor?" she demanded. "Who was it? They ain't *never* meant to hit a girl."

"I hit first," I said, staring at my shoes.

She blinked at me. "Now why did you do that?"

I was silent for a long moment, struggling to hold back all the furious thoughts in my head, a swarm of angry wasps just waiting for somebody to punch a hole in their nest. I spat half a mouthful of blood onto the ground, scuffed it out with my foot. "They were sayin' things."

"What kinda things?"

"About my daddy," I mumbled. "Said he's never comin' home, he found some other woman and he ain't comin' back." A bead of sweat rolled down my neck. "They were makin' fun of your mama, too. I can't even say it, it was so bad."

Jessie nodded, her chin jutting out. "So you hit 'em."

"It was a great shot," I said solemnly. "Kept my thumb out, just like your daddy taught us. Didn't hurt a bit."

She was fighting back a smile, I knew it, but she just took my right hand in hers, inspecting my scraped knuckles. "You sure this didn't hurt?"

"Sure I'm sure," I said. "Don't think they broke my nose, either. It's just bleedin' real good."

"What a baby," said Jessie, her eyes glittering. "You tell your nose to quit it. Nobody's got any pity."

"Nobody? Well, that's a damn shame," I said. "On account of it hurts an awful lot, and seein' how it got this hurt when I was defendin' our honor—"

"Oh, no you don't," she cut in. "I never asked nobody to fight for me, don't you go makin' me feel guilty—"

I kissed her then, on her mouth and teeth. She pulled back and wrinkled her nose. She said, "You taste like blood."

I waited, watching her. Already feeling my left eye begin to swell up. Jessie sighed, the tiniest of noises, and leaned in to kiss me short and quick. Like I knew she would.

"Oh!" I yanked away from her, hands flying to my face. "Oh goddammit, Jessie, my fuckin' nose!"

"Not my fault either," she sang, but she took me back to her house and sat me down at the table, washed all the blood and snot off my face with a wet cloth, and she was so gentle I almost cried. It wasn't the first fight I ever got into, and it wouldn't be the last. I was not a soft or tender thing. Sometimes it felt like my chest was a windowpane, and my heart was a clenched fist beating against it. All I could do was spit shards of broken glass, and she would catch them in her hands.

Thatch and me reach the ocean right before sunset, after two straight days of leading the poor horses through thick marshland, the mud sucking at their hooves, the wet heat slumping over our shoulders. To be honest, I don't even figure out we're close until we're already there. First I hear this odd sound, somehow like whispers and rolling thunder at the same time, and then we trot past the last line of swamp grass onto the sandy shore.

Thatch says, "Like nothin' you ever seen, huh."

Like nothin' I ever seen, that's for sure. It's almost frightening—the unimaginable size of it. The ocean mirrors the sky, a curve of blue stretching out to brush the horizon, flecked with white where the waves break. I slide off my horse without a word, grabbing my bag and sprinting forward across the loose sand until my feet hit the tide. I feel it soaking my boots, but all I can think is that my lips taste like salt and the water is cool against my legs and it's time, it's time, it's time.

I reach into my bag and pull out a little ball of cloth. It used to be blue, but over thirteen years it faded to pale gray, the color of a snowy sky in Boston. The cloth unfurls like a flower in my hand, and there, in the center: a single pearly tooth. She gave it to me when we were eight years old and losing the last of our baby teeth. She pressed it into my palm like a secret, like a tiny, shining promise.

This is all I have left of her.

"Flora," she said, tongue thick, words slow as molasses, "Flor, I just thought of the funniest thing," and I said, "What's that?" and she started to say something but pulled up short. Her mouth snapped shut with a click.

"What's the funniest thing, Jessie, tell me," I said, patting her face. We were twenty years old and looked like we'd been dipped in stardust. When the world ended.

"I—oh," she said, frowning a little. "I feel strange. I feel real strange all of a sudden."

"What kinda strange?" I asked. I was still half-smiling, overcome with the glory of it all. It was April in Boston, the snow mostly melted away, spring rain bringing fog and slick streets. Tonight some burly man had bet a dollar that us two pretty girls couldn't outdrink him. So we were a dollar rich.

"No, no, Flor, I'm...I'm not laughin', I feel..." Jessie was stock-still, confusion written all over her face, one hand fluttering near her temple. Then, "Oh," she said almost wonderingly, and she dropped to her knees so fast the ice on the street cracked beneath her, this horrible *snap*, and I just about stopped breathing.

Turned out Jessie's mama gave her a sickness. After that, we had eleven months, two weeks, and four days.

Never said the world ended quick.

I think Thatch walks up beside me, or maybe he tethers the horses. I'm not really sure. All I can do is stand there, the ocean licking at my skirts, holding Jessamine's little tooth as gently as I can, cradling it in my hand like a child.

"Dear God," I begin, but my throat closes, and I can't get any further. I don't think she'll mind. She was always better at talking out loud, better at finding the right spots to bury those cow bones, better at crying for creatures and people and anything that needed her tears. So I just clutch her tooth, that last precious piece of her, and bring it to my forehead, my chest, my left shoulder and then my right. I kneel down right there in the shallow tide and dig her a little hole. I press her into the thick wet sand and cover her up, right as the breaking waves surge up to meet her.

Dear God, I pray silently, *she kissed the blood off my mouth. Dear God, she did that for me. So I will love her. I will love her like a bullet loves a man's chest, all the way down to the bone, hard and unforgiving. Pain in every breath. I have, and I will.*

And Jesus Christ, it has counted for something.

I stare out at that wide expanse of ocean, gleaming gold beneath the sinking sun, the white-capped waves crawling forward across the sand over and over again, and I listen to the ancient rush and roar of it, and I think: *Look, Jessie. Here it is.*

New Millennium Nonfiction Award

Karen Hunt

INTO THE WORLD

Karen Hunt's writing is inspired by her travels to over fifty countries and her experiences living in England, Switzerland, France, and Slovenia. In a world increasingly divided by violence and fear, Karen is committed to connecting children from diverse cultures through her MY WORLD PROJECT.

She is the co-founder of InsideOUT Writers, a creative writing program for incarcerated youth, and the only female boxing and kick-boxing trainer at a gritty L.A. boxing gym.

The first book in her YA Urban Fantasy series, *Night Angels Chronicles*, is soon to be released by Evernight Teen. She is the author and/or illustrator of nineteen children's books (many under the name Mezek Leimert) and has written numerous essays about raising kids as a single mom. Her greatest inspirations are, and forever will be, her three children and two grandchildren.

You can follow Karen's adventures at *khmezek.com* and connect with her on Twitter *@karenalainehunt*.

*I*T IS APPROPRIATE THAT *I received news of this award as I was on my way to Marrakech. Writing* INTO THE WORLD *has been a lesson in endurance, working on it when I can, because it is something I am compelled to write. And I can say that this magical part of the world, Morocco and Egypt in particular, were perhaps the biggest influences in my life from those childhood traveling adventures. So for many years, I kept that dream alive, that determination to come to Morocco and to finish the book. I am blessed to have that dream become a reality, with the added bonus of being able to work with children while I am here.*

I am a traveler and I travel where and when I can, through words and pictures and through mountains and valleys and cities and villages. This is a gift that I have been given and I am grateful, although it can be a burden to be so driven, and I do not take the responsibility lightly. When I write, I do it with my whole heart and mind. It is my way of knowing that I exist and that what I do on this planet matters. My hope for INTO THE WORLD, *and everything I write, is that it will fight against irrational hysteria and turn people's consciousness away from fear towards unity.*

We are all strangers in a strange land, even inside our own skin. We can never truly know ourselves or even those who are closest to us, but that doesn't stop us from trying, each in our own ways. And so life is essentially a lesson in the acceptance of loneliness, whether we live surrounded by loved ones or on an isolated mountaintop. Understanding that we are all in this same predicament is, ironically, what gives us compassion towards one another and brings us closer together.

—Karen Hunt

INTO THE WORLD

Karen Hunt

EXCERPT: REFLECTIONS FROM ISTANBUL

Istanbul, July 2014

I WAS TEN YEARS OLD when my dad heard the voice of God telling him to give up his business career and become a writer. He gathered our family of six into his study, randomly opened his Bible, pointed at a verse and read, "Go ye into all the world and preach the Gospel." Then, he raised his eyes, aflame with fervor, and said, "That is what we are going to do."

It was the turbulent sixties and it might have seemed the height of folly to give up everything that was safe and secure to head off for the unknown with only God's voice to lead us. Yet not to my parents. They always obeyed God's voice, as interpreted by my dad. So we packed our bags and boarded a plane for London, the idea being that we would travel for at least a year, and that our adventures would inspire my dad's writing. We were to be ambassadors of the Lord, spreading God's light in the darkness. We should be "IN THE WORLD BUT NOT OF IT"—that was the calling of all devout Christians.

Last summer, I returned to Istanbul to write, remembering how forty-eight years earlier my family had fled across the border from Syria into Turkey just as the Six-Day War was starting, a mere few hours before the borders were closed. On June 6, the official start of the war, I celebrated my eleventh birthday in Ankara, my family seeking news of the conflict with dread.

During this most recent visit to Istanbul, I stayed in a penthouse flat just off Istiklal Cadessi, with a view of the Bosporus and the giant ships sailing in and out of port. Once while sitting in my favorite café, I watched the riot police go by, and then a group of running protestors, unable to stop myself from following after them. Listening to their voices singing for peace, I could not have anticipated that I would return home to news of the fatal killings by police of unarmed Michael Brown and Eric Garner and a nation in turmoil. And right now, as I write this, I am reading of Freddie Gray's death in the back of a police van, the result of a "Nickel Ride," a torture practiced by police where a suspect is handcuffed in the back of a van without a seat belt and driven recklessly around town.

Sitting on my terrace in the evening with a glass of wine, I had the uneasy feeling that nothing much had changed in the ensuing years. The summer of 2014 saw the war in Gaza explode onto the world stage, ISIS become the new Satan, and Malaysia Airline flight M17 shot down over the Ukraine. Walking to get my coffee one morning, I encountered boys playing in the streets with guns, under the benevolent gaze of old men hunched on chairs and gossiping and drinking tea. "Free Gaza" posters had sprung up overnight, plastered on buildings everywhere.

There has never been any shortage of enemies to fight out there in the big wide world. Now more than ever, the evil terrorists, those fundamentalist crazies who are endangering all the Christian principles upon which the United States has been founded, can be battled not only in the field but on social media. How is it possible that so many could hate us so much?

A better question is: *how could they not?*

I have a long history of traveling the world and experiencing the dangers that go with it. In the eighties I lived in London and in Tito's Yugoslavia. In London, terrorism was an everyday concern. One morning, upon arriving at the corner shop on Bayswater to buy my daily newspaper, I found that it had been blown to pieces. Looking out for suspicious packages on buses and trains was a natural part of life. In the Slovenian village where I spent my summers, I heard stories of the hatred that had been brewing to the South for hundreds of years and which, sure enough, exploded to the surface after Tito's death.

When I visited my family in Los Angeles and saw the excess and heard how people raved about President Reagan, I wondered how Americans could be so ignorant of what was going on in the rest of the world, the common perception being that United States was despised because people from other countries were jealous of us. All those foreigners were hypocrites, complaining about our materialism while watching our movies and drinking our Coke. The United States was the richest country on earth and we had the possessions to prove it. Obviously, they wanted to be just like us—hell, they wanted to *be* us. My friends and family didn't see the dangers, not to the mention the absurdity, of this one-dimensional attitude. If I ever dared suggest that I understood why so many people of other nations despised us, I was quickly shut down as unpatriotic and corrupted by living abroad.

In 1966, I was a naïve kid under the subjugation of my fundamentalist Christian parents. I didn't question what I was told: that my religion and my country were righteous and good and that God was on our side. I was raised a Plymouth Brethren. Not a lot of people know what that means, but Rebecca West, a favorite author of mine, made a biting comment about it in an interview with *The Paris Review, The Art of Fiction, No. 65.* She said her paternal grandmother "was a member of the Plymouth Brethren and a religious fanatic with a conscience that should have been held down and, you know, eunuchized or castrated." I completely appreciate this description. Religious fanatics are tormented by a conscience at war with itself, telling them they must do right and good while at the same time telling them that they will never be right or good enough. And so they must continually justify themselves, while castigating everyone else as beneath them.

Christians are going to heaven and heathens are going to hell. Conservative fundamentalists are raised on the Book of Revelation. It is drilled into us that after the Rapture, God's Faithful Army will return with Christ to massacre the infidels who remain on earth. What this means is that if you are a Christian mother, for example, and your child is not a Christian, you will come back and run that child through with the sword without any compunction. At the same time, we are taught to "love" those infidels with a love so pure that mundane concerns such as feeding and clothing the poor can only be important if they lead to "saving souls."

Never would it have occurred to me that such a mindset was not much different from that of fundamentalists from other religions. I didn't question the inconsistencies, not to mention the absolute horror of such beliefs, at the beginning of our trip. But by the end of it, the way I saw the world and the people in it would be far removed from the precepts upon which I had been raised.

August 16, 1966, we boarded a plane for London, the first time I would be leaving my safe and well-intentioned world. I didn't know that on August 1, 1966, an ex-marine named Charles Witman had killed sixteen in a bloody rampage at the University of Texas. I didn't know that on August 5, Dr. Martin Luther King, Jr. was stoned during a Chicago march. Or that race riots had broken out in Lansing Michigan on August 7. I didn't know the darker truths of my nation. I was firm in my faith that we were the good guys and the people we would encounter on our travels were heathens.

But then I met those heathens. And when I think of meeting them and how they changed my perspective, I think especially of a certain Nubian sailor in Egypt, and a young boy on a mountainous road in Turkey.

Egypt, May 1967

We'd crossed a choppy sea by ferry from Greece and were excited to reach Egypt.

Egypt!

Land of the pharaohs, pyramids, enchantment, romance—ha! It took forever to get off the boat, even with the self-appointed "official" who attached himself to us, demanding ten dollars for his services. A horrifying amount, my mother thought, but she was gratified to see that once money was exchanged, things began to happen. Our official was now our loyal defender, going so far as to physically assault any other "official" who dared to come near us.

It was a relief to finally get inside our VW van and on the road, although all sense of safety or security vanished when we noticed the guards armed with machine guns patrolling the streets. Newly installed artillery could be seen along the waterfront. At every intersection the grainy voice of Nasser spouted from P.A. systems, denouncing Israel, accompanied by frenzied applause from the crowds.

We drove to Cairo on a dusty desert route lined with crumbling flat-roofed dwellings or tents, and here and there a camel or a donkey, dejected, head hanging low. It was an odious drive, continually interrupted by checkpoints, impossible to tell which were official and which weren't. Along the loneliest stretch of road, an officer suddenly jumped out of a moving army truck just ahead of us, imperiously flagged us down and, to our astonishment, jumped into our car. He rode with us into Cairo, asking questions about what we thought of Egypt and Nasser, to which our parents replied diplomatically.

We were greatly relieved to see him go and even more relieved to reach our Cairo youth hostel. Once in our room, we threw open the windows to the most chaotic and intimidating city we were to experience on our travels. Donkeys, camels, chickens, pedestrians, bicyclists, merchants hawking their wares, buses, dilapidated trucks, and rickety smog-pelting cars all vied for space on the streets and sidewalks. In fact, the sidewalks seemed to be equally considered a place on which to drive as the pock-marked streets. A constant barrage of horns, angry voices, and barking, bleating, and braying animals left me confused and disoriented.

In her journal, my mom described the city as having a "holiday air" as it prepared to fight. The papers were filled with references to the evil aggressor, the United States, and Israel being the "stooge" of the Imperialists. As Mom so astutely observed, "While the people themselves are friendly on an individual level, they are united by hatred of Jews and of the U.S., and a holy war seems imminent, to annihilate Israel."

We were excited to find a store with books in English, although we were confused to see that they were published in Moscow. My mom picked up an oversized photography book about the United States, expecting to see beautiful pictures of scenery and impressive cities. Instead it was filled with photos of ghettos and claims that we were a "Gangster State" and Israel was our "Gangster Stooge." On closer inspection, we realized that most of the books were filled with propaganda against our wonderful country. Mom was incensed and complained to the clerk, who was Russian: "How can you publish these lies? How can you claim that in America 'a few billionaires live in palaces and control and exploit the country, compared to the rest of the people who live in miserable shacks crowded into narrow streets with no trees?'" The clerk remained stone-faced and disdainful. My mom shook her head and we all walked out in a unified huff.

None of us were sorry to leave Cairo behind, as we traveled south along the Nile to Luxor and the Valley of the Kings. On this tortuous road of four hundred miles, we met only one other foreigner—going in the opposite direction. We waved and honked, feeling more alone for having seen him. Gone were the army trucks and the screaming voice of Nasser and the mindless crowds. Instead, fields of golden grain stretched out before us, bent figures cutting it with short knives and gathering it into sheaves. The road often became no more than a dirt camel path, yet children would suddenly appear out of nowhere, running alongside our car and yelling for money and candy. Stopping at a ramshackle food stand, hot bodies pressed up close to inspect us, I came face to face with girls my age with thick, dark hair and open mouths, staring wide-eyed, as if I were a movie star.

At last we made it to Luxor, excited to stay in our only experience of a first-class hotel, the Savoy. After all those youth hostels, we expected this to be the best night of our lives thus far.

What a disappointment. The air-conditioning didn't work. The toilets didn't work. There was no hot water.

"I wouldn't mind so much," said Mom severely, "if it weren't for the 'Nasser folders' that they have on the bedside table. Listen to this!" And she read from the folder that described Egypt as the wonder of the world for its beautiful blending of the past with the even more glorious present.

That night, the air grew insufferably still and suffocating, and we dragged a mattress onto the balcony hoping for a breeze. There was no relief from the mosquitoes, though, which brutally attacked us and buzzed in our ears. My last impression before sleep finally carried me away was of the Nile bathed in moonlight, the savage barking of wild dogs floating across the river.

When the Nubian approached us in the hotel lobby the next morning and offered to take us for a sail on the Nile in his felucca, our parents said yes, while I wanted to scream no. It was too hot, the bites on my body too painful. I just wanted to lie down somewhere and wallow in misery, dreaming of hamburgers and french fries and my own bed and bathroom.

"Ah, you can be relaxing on the boat," said the Nubian, as if reading my mind. "Never you see anything so beautiful, so peaceful." Somehow, his noble, graceful movements and melodious voice silenced further protests, and off we went.

Once on the boat, I forgot all about my homesickness and the bites. It was always like that, yearning for comfort and familiarity one moment and then suddenly an onslaught of extraordinary beauty, sites, smells, and sounds hitting me and exhilaration overcoming my depression. I wanted to float along forever, the breeze that I had so craved filling the sail and gliding us forward, bringing relief from the still heat of the shore. The boat was old but sturdy, as if it had sailed back and forth for a thousand years and no storm or drought could conquer it. The man was thin and sinewy, the veins showing on his forearms, so shiny-black against the white of his robes. He looked like an extension of everything around him, as if he had grown out of the earth itself.

The Nubian's robes flapped in a sudden breeze and he grasped them between his teeth as he expertly maneuvered the sails. I wondered how he put on his turban and if he didn't get hot under it. Anyway, what *was* under it? Hair or a bald head? I didn't dare ask.

I felt suddenly shy as I realized he was smiling at me.

"You like this sailing, yes?"

I nodded, unable to speak.

"Let me tell you of this Nile, so important for us," he said, his black eyes shifting from me to the far horizon, as if he saw the past and present all as one. "The king in reign of Ramesses III, 20th dynasty, he and all royalty sail down this Nile from Karnak to Temple of Luxor. In this most important temple rite, the king and his Ka, that is to say, uh…his divine essence created at birth…unite into one and he become divine being. Crowds, they cheer, be very happy, running beside this river. They be given much loaves of bread. Beautiful, happy celebration. So now, you, young lady from United States of America, you be queen, sailing in royal boat to unite with Ka, become immortal, yes?"

I liked that image. Me, a queen. "Do you believe those old stories, that they're true?"

The Nubian threw back his head and laughed, then raised his hands joyously to the heavens. "I believe in Allah, merciful, compassionate, just. This is truth. This is what I know."

We continued to sail lazily along. The Nubian motioned towards an upturned barrel and I sat on it.

"I tell you a story, yes?" he said.

I settled down happily. To sail the Nile, listening to a robed and turbaned Nubian tell a story—what could be better?

"A man, he live in my village, born with crossed eyes, never looking straight. Always, the old ladies whisper, ohhh, they say, he has devil inside! They say if he look at you with one eye, the other looking in opposite direction, he steal your soul, taking it in one eye and out the other into underworld. For this reason, since a little boy until a grown man, he was outcast from village, sent to live in reeds and mud, no home. One day, a little girl, she fall in river and the cross-eyed one, he save her. You think the people thank him, yes? But no, they only hate him more. They stone him then, say he throw her in this river, try to drown her. No matter it not be true. You see, people for so long make him something evil, it then impossible to say, oh, excuse us, we be wrong. So, when he show them how good he is, they just be more angry. The little girl, she grow up and move away from the village. She go to Alexandria, go to college. She become a writer and make a story of cross-eyed man and people hear this story and it help them live better life. So, I ask you: Was that man with cross eyes lucky or no?"

"I don't think so," I said, pretty sure I was giving the wrong answer though I couldn't think of why.

The Nubian threw up his hands and laughed more joyously than ever. "Allah be praised! He was lucky! He save girl who go on to make his story in words. And his story teach many good lessons. So, forever in story he live. Maybe he suffer in life, but he live *forever*. So, I ask you: If you rather have easy life and disappear to nothing, or suffering life and live on in stories?"

"I don't really want to suffer," I said truthfully.

The Nubian's white teeth gleamed, the smile engulfing his face. "Life is suffering."

How, I wondered, could he smile like that while uttering such a bleak statement? This was something I would struggle to comprehend for many years to come.

It was hard to say goodbye to the Nubian, but when the moment came, he bowed solemnly, his hands clasped together as if in prayer. I bowed back.

"Allah be with you," he said.

"And God be with you," I said. We both smiled. Then he turned and strode proudly back to his felucca.

Back at our hotel, sitting outside on our balcony and swatting at the interminable mosquitoes, I asked my dad about Allah.

He was sternly emphatic. "Allah is the devil and those who believe in him are destined for hell."

"But our guide was such a good man, I can't see him in hell," I argued.

"Karen, you know people can only be saved by asking Jesus into their hearts."

Long after I lay down, hot and sweaty and unable to sleep, I thought and thought about what it all must mean. Why did I have such subversive thoughts? I simply could not accept that the Nubian was going to hell. I'd never met anyone who deserved to go to heaven more than he did.

It was sad leaving the land of the Nubian, but not the land of Nasser. Our last morning in Cairo we awoke to find the entire city plastered in posters of red and black Arabic, which it was probably better we couldn't read. Our desire had been to get to Israel but every time my dad asked at the travel bureau, they screamed back—and I mean *screamed*, "Israel does not exist!" Screaming was beneath my dad, but he did respond in a loud and commanding voice that carried throughout the vast room, "Yes, it does!" He was so brave, so sure in his convictions. I felt like such a coward, terrified that his claims would get us all killed.

As much as Dad believed it was God's will we go to Israel, he had no choice but to book passage on a boat to Beirut and we sailed to Lebanon, arriving on May 29.

We settled into a charming coastal bungalow for just six dollars, realizing that the rest of the bungalows were ominously empty of tourists. And so we found ourselves stuck in this beautiful place, our tension growing with each passing day. There were no ships except back to Alexandria. We reached the conclusion that our only way out was through Syria into Turkey. It wasn't part of our plan, but if war started, our lives wouldn't be worth much in this part of the world.

Once in Syria, we passed through villages built in the shadows of mountaintop crusader castles, the people looking at us with curious surprise. I had never felt so conspicuous or alone. There were no other tourists, no one else foolhardy enough to be stuck in this part of the world during such a dangerous time. We reached Latakia, the last town before the border into Turkey. The streets were lined with men carrying bayonets, mouths unsmiling beneath luxuriant mustaches, eyes fixed on us, and my skin crawled with fear. Driving slowly through the narrow streets, we felt

naked and exposed in our fire engine-red van, but managed
to pass through without incident, making it to the border
before sundown. Later we discovered that it was only a
matter of hours before the borders were closed.

Turkey, June 1967

Once in Turkey, it was as if we'd been holding our breath
for days and could finally release it. We wound through
cool pine forests, past tumbling streams bordered by wild
oleander, suddenly opening into high valleys of waving
grasslands, mingled with wildflowers, craggy outcrops, and
then more mountains and valleys beyond.

As we traveled a lonely mountain road, the setting sun
painting the sky in a fiery glow, we came upon a little proces-
sion, appearing magically as if out of nowhere.

Mom clapped her hands in delight. "It looks like
a courtship."

A young woman, dressed in her finest gown, gold coins
dangling from her forehead, ears, and neck, walked beside
a young man, dressed in his finest suit. Both were strolling
lazily and chewing on long strings of sweet grass. Behind
them, at a discrete distance, rode a woman on a donkey,
with a young boy walking beside her.

"No doubt her mother and brother. Chaperones,"
said Mom.

We waved as we drove past and they waved back, the
young woman sweetly shy, her cheeks rosy, the young man
leaning towards her instinctively, possessively. The mother
on the donkey slapped her thigh with a switch in merriment
and the boy ran after our car, waving his arms and yelling
something we couldn't understand.

I hung out the window, waved, and yelled back, "Have a nice life! God bless you!"

He sped up, trying to catch us but couldn't. Finally he gave up and stopped running. I continued to watch as he grew smaller and smaller and then disappeared entirely as we rounded a corner.

Maybe our paths would cross again someday. Maybe twenty years from now, we'd both be in a restaurant or an airport. Maybe in Tanzania or Venezuela or New York. We'd be grown up and we wouldn't recognize each other. We wouldn't know that many years before we had waved and laughed and exchanged words we couldn't understand on a lonely mountain road, the sky on fire above us.

At Antakya we were welcomed like superstars, as if we'd been expected, the roadside lined with greeters who waved and shouted us into town, the only tourists to have come out of Syria. Such a difference from the border town of Syria, where we'd been afraid of bayonets piercing our lungs. Strange, so strange! What made it different? We weren't any different. The people in either town weren't any different. But in Syria, circumstances had forced us to react to one another with suspicion and dread, whereas here we were all friends who could embrace one another without fear. It just went to show how ridiculous, how stupid and ignorant war was.

My birthday was celebrated in Ankara, but it wasn't much of a celebration. We listened for news, trying to decipher what must be true and what wasn't. Jerusalem was in flames, Cairo bombed and the American Embassy burned, an Israeli plane downed in Lebanon, bodies piling up. Israel had overrun Sinai and taken Suez. A great victory. But at what terrible cost?

"Maybe some of the very ones who were kind to us are dead," Mom worried.

On June 12 we left Turkey and entered the Communist Block at Bulgaria. We were on our next mission: to smuggle bibles into Romania. My dad had a contact to give the bibles to, just like a spy in a thriller. Only there was nothing romantic or spy-worthy about smuggling bibles. And yet we could be imprisoned for doing it. Just one more righteous act we were performing in order to save lost souls from hell.

Home

In the summer of 1967, our marvelous trip ended and we sailed across the Atlantic and began the long cross-country journey home. I was surprised at the emotions welling up inside of me. I wanted so badly to get home, sleep once again in my own bed, and see my friends. Nothing would have changed, would it? Desperately I wanted to believe that nothing would have changed. To have come so far, to have crossed the stormy ocean and then still have to travel across a continent to reach my home was almost unbearable.

Traversing the southern states, I only remember cockroaches as big as my fist, or so they seemed to me, and once, getting out at a gas station in a town that boasted a sign—"Friendliest God-fearing Town on Earth"—terribly thirsty, and approaching the drinking fountain to find a sign in bold black letters: "Whites Only."

That sign stopped me cold. I didn't know what to do. I'd been in many countries where I'd feared drinking the water because it might make my body sick. But never a fear like this. Never a fear that if I drank this water, my spirit would become infected with a disease far worse than any bodily ill. How could I drink from such a fountain?

It seemed worse than walking through Dachau and seeing the ovens and the pictures of all those suffering millions. Well it wasn't *worse*, there was no way to make a comparison. But that at least had been a walk through the past, ghosts and bones left as reminders so that we as conscious human beings could learn and change our ways. Yes, Dachau was a story to be told so that it would never be forgotten, hopefully not relived.

But this, in my own country, was real, right now, in front of my face. I stood rooted to the ground, the heat from the pavement searing my feet through my thin sandals, unable to move. I stood as surely as I had stood in front of the Berlin Wall, a wall that had claimed the lives of so many trying to escape to freedom. Here, too, was a wall enslaving an entire race of people. It was an Evil, as vile and insidious as anything that had happened down through history. This reality that confronted me was not yet a story to be told, a story to be learned from. It was happening right now—I was experiencing it in my home-land, in my world.

At last I could stand my thirst no longer, and I drank from the fountain. It came down to a physical need, no longer moral or philosophical. The water was cool and refreshing as it ran down my throat. It did what it was supposed to do: quenched my thirst. What about the man or woman who craved water in this God-forsaken land but did not dare approach? And it was a God-forsaken land, no matter how many bible-thumping churches were spread across the towns and cities. It was God-forsaken to have a sign like that, plain as day and no one thinking twice about it. What was the difference between one person and another? We all got thirsty. We all cried and laughed about the same things, wished and hoped for the same things.

I remembered the Nubian sailor, his face chiseled as if from obsidian, long robe billowing behind him as he stood proud and tall, guiding his boat through the water. He had shown me profound beauty in the flow of the river, the bending of the reeds, the curve of the banks, the unbearable blueness of the sky. In those few hours he had enlightened me in ways that all my hours in church had not.

What about the boy in Turkey who had waved at me on that country road and to whom I had felt such a connection? Was he going to hell, just because he had been born there instead of in my neighborhood?

I felt ashamed that my thirst had overcome my convictions. Couldn't I have been stronger? Couldn't I have *done* something? At least, I could have torn down the sign and *then* taken a drink. But to what end? I was just one person. I supposed there were many like me who came to the fountain, disapproved of what they saw, but drank anyway, rationalizing their actions by thinking that they were just one person.

And that is the problem: we all think we are just "one person." And we are. But one person can start a revolution of thought and action. Still standing in front of the fountain, not yet able to turn away from what I had done, I thought of what kind of courage it took for someone of color to bend down and drink. Certainly more courage than it took for me *not* to drink, and I hadn't even accomplished that much.

I thought of Dr. Martin Luther King, Jr. He had that kind of courage. His voice had risen against the tide, compelling people to rise up with him. Less than one year later, that voice of searing truth would be silenced by an assassin's bullet. But of course, I didn't know that then.

I turned from the fountain and headed back to the car. A hot breeze kicked up dust and a miniature tornado whirled dizzily past, carrying debris along with it. The owner of the gas station, a beefy fellow in bleached overalls, waved at me and smiled. He seemed nice—and he *was* nice, that's what made life so maddening.

"Your daddy told me about your journey. You must be dying to get home, young lady."

I nodded. Yes, I was.

"Have a souvenir from the friendliest, most God-fearing town on earth," he said, clearly oblivious to the irony of that statement. He handed me a miniature New Testament, shiny-black with gold-trimmed pages, and I was too timid to refuse, not wanting to see his nice façade fall away and the judgment appear.

Driving through the deserts of Nevada, profound beauty that made me gasp with wonder, it dawned on me what I would find at the end of my journey. I had desperately wanted to return home to my comfortable, familiar world and find it exactly the same as when I'd left. And so it would be. But the thing was, *I* was different. My experiences had opened my mind and heart to the wonders of the world, and I had embraced all of it.

We passed through Las Vegas and my parents actually made us avert our gaze from the city of sin. Arriving in Los Angeles at last, the city lights twinkling at dusk, I made a resolution. I might only be one person but I would do something with my life to change the world. I would stand up against wrong. It was a tall order, an enthusiastic commitment made by a young girl with very little understanding of the impact such a resolution would have on her life.

But we all must start somewhere. There must be a place where we draw that line in the sand and then consciously step over it, embracing our journey, no matter the consequences.

There must be a time when we tear down the sign and invite everyone to drink from the fountain.

The 39th

New Millennium Nonfiction Award

Susan Nathiel

HEARING SILENCE

Susan Nathiel grew up in Oklahoma with a scientist father who wrote textbooks and a mentally ill mother who wrote poetry. Thanks to them, she became both a psychotherapist and a writer, publishing *Daughters of Madness* and *Sons of Madness*. She lives in rural Connecticut with her family, who yield the front porch swing to her when she's writing.

*S*INCE I'VE BEEN A *psychotherapist for over thirty years, I know a lot about how people react to trauma. After the first few waves of shock subside, which can take years, there are still things that you just can't get to lie flat on the page. It's amazing how long you can turn something over and over in your mind and never get anywhere different with it. Maybe those particular moments stand for the whole thing, or maybe they're the ones that happen the moment before you're shattered.*

This piece was a long time in the writing, and it took me places I didn't anticipate. Years after the event of my brother's death, I was still stuck with the question I pose in "Hearing Silence," and I couldn't shake it. Writing made me stay with the question long enough for the answer to show up on the page, and by the time I got there, it just wrote itself. I looked down at what I had written and I knew it was the truth. For me, then, writing is a way to say what I know, but it's also a way to discover what wants to be written whether I know it or not.

—Susan Nathiel

HEARING SILENCE

Susan Nathiel

On that hot september day in 1986, when we buried my brother Chris, our parents did not speak to each other. It wasn't due to grief, or guilt, or blame. It was due to me. They had only seen each other twice since their divorce sixteen years earlier, and there had been little drama. Yet that day, I kept them apart as though they were unstable nuclear elements. I did it without thinking, without a moment's hesitation. Even now, over twenty years later, I still wonder why I interfered, since you might think any two parents, divorced or not, would have a right to speak to each other at their son's funeral. Of the two questions that have lingered all this time, that's the one that's mine alone to answer.

My brother had been uncharacteristically quiet on the question of how we should deal with his death, how we should understand what happened and why. He hadn't left a note.

A month before his funeral, my brother was told that unless he agreed to an admission at a psychiatric hospital for impaired physicians, he would be out of a job and might lose his license. In his case, "impaired" was a euphemism for depression and prescription drug abuse, none of which I knew about at the time.

We had never been very close. Chris was four years older than me, David was in the middle, and I was "Suze," the little sister. He was the "smart one," who made up in academic achievement what he lacked in adolescent cool. He was a know-it-all who showed only occasional big-brother kindnesses. Once, when I was sick for weeks, he came to my bedroom to read me my favorite *Cowboy Bob* book. I was too young to read it myself and he usually teased me because I carried it with me everywhere, longing to find someone patient enough to read it to me again, despite my knowing every word by heart. This one time, he pulled a chair up close to my bed, and read it to me page by page, letting me gaze at the familiar pictures. It was my fondest memory of him.

As adults, we barely kept in touch even though we presumably had things in common: he had become a psychiatrist and I a family therapist. On a rare visit, I went to see him in Utah a few years before his death. That one time, we actually talked to each other and he told me for the first time about his long struggle with depression. He had gained weight from the medications, and his puffy face was stiff and wooden. His heavy-lidded eyes opened into a well of sadness I didn't want to see; I preferred to believe him when he said he was feeling better.

I knew from my visit that he was regarded as an excellent psychiatrist, even though he was privately picking and choosing his own mix of drugs. Like many doctors, he had relied on uppers and downers in med school, but he had kept going long afterwards, and eventually wasn't able to hide the effects from his colleagues. For a while he was erratically up and down, his mind zooming all over the place like a remote-controlled model airplane with no one at the controls. Then the downs became more pronounced, and when his slow walk became a shuffle, and he fell asleep in meetings every afternoon, he was finally given the ultimatum about his job.

At the San Diego psychiatric hospital, their first plan was to take him off everything to get an idea of his baseline. Chris had protested that the old depression would return if he stopped all his medications, but they also had a plan B: they wanted him to try electroshock therapy (ECT).

Electroshock, though, was not a good plan. Our mother had been hospitalized and given shock therapy when we were children and again later, when I was fifteen and Chris was away at college. We never mentioned these things, much less discussed them. They were gaps in the narrative of our family life, things we pretended not to notice at the time, then simply omitted from the story later on.

After his death, I came across an autobiography Chris had written for a therapist after his first serious depression, in medical school. He had not forgotten those gaps. He had written:

> *My life was shattered at the age of six. One of my most vivid memories was that horrible day when my mother became psychotic. She had often been sad before...she used to cry on my shoulder when I barely came up to her waist. In retrospect, I feel that if I had only done or said the right thing perhaps I could have saved my mother. I know these feelings sound ridiculous, and the notion of a six-year-old boy saving his mother from a major psychiatric illness sounds preposterous, but nevertheless that is the way I feel. Somehow I failed her in a very tragic way.*

"That is the way I feel," he had written, in the present tense.

On the day things really got bad, I was supposed to have a report card from first grade signed by my mother and then take it to school. My mother was in a peculiar state in which she was unable to move. She stayed in one position and could not or would not speak to me and could not move...I was terrified and went to school without my report card being signed and was obviously very upset. When I returned from school my mother had been taken away, I later learned, to the psychiatric ward of the general hospital. I also learned later that she had been given electroshock treatment during the weeks she was away.

When she returned home, it seemed as if she was no longer my mother. I am unable to express how important this occurrence is in my life. It is difficult for you or anyone to imagine the impact on a small child of seeing his mother in such a bizarre state, then having her taken away for a lengthy period of time with no understanding of what the problem was. I recall...feeling it might have been better for her to die, to disappear forever, than come back seemingly a different person.

In the hospital, as Chris came off all the medications, the old depression was indeed still there. That meant the ECT part of the plan loomed. Then, ten days into his stay, he received a letter from his wife Dianne, saying she was taking the kids up to Carson City, Nevada for a couple of weeks to stay with her mother. She assured him that they'd be back, but just needed a break before school started. Chris's eleven-year-old stepson, Chuck, had been deeply affected by the hospitalization; Chris and Dianne's daughter Heather, only four, seemed happy enough, but stuck by her mother's side a little too much. Dianne also wrote a letter to Chris's psychiatrist, saying she was worried about Chris's reaction, and asking that they keep a close watch on him for a while.

It's still a mystery how he was able to get a one-hour pass to go into town only days after that letter, when he was considered a possible risk to himself. Maybe he was persuasive. Maybe somebody didn't read the precautions in his chart. Maybe they thought he was better. At any rate, he exited the hospital with the pass, his wallet, and a plan of his own.

First he went to the nearest airport, where he bought a ticket and flew to Salt Lake City. Then he rented a car and drove to the outskirts of Orem, the small town where he and his family had lived for several years. At the K-Mart in a shopping mall, he used his MasterCard to buy a garment bag, a box of shells, and a 12-gauge shotgun. They sold firearms over the counter in Utah then, no questions asked. Then he drove to a motel and checked in, using his real name. I wondered later what they thought of him, a tall middle-aged fellow, soft-spoken, with old acne scars and thick glasses. He would have been polite but probably insistent about wanting a quiet room, away from others. He would have seemed like any overnight guest, carrying the garment bag over his shoulder, walking away down the hall, disappearing into the elevator.

In the room he waited, evidently for a couple of hours. For what? For whom? If he was waiting for someone to try to find him, he had no way of knowing that the hospital hadn't even noticed his absence yet. Or perhaps it just took time to get up his nerve.

In this particular room there was a narrow entry hall just a few feet long and about three feet wide, which opened into the bedroom area on one side and the bathroom on the other. Despite the day of travel, and the waiting, he hadn't washed his hands; the towels and washcloths were all in place, folded over in neat motel triangles.

Sometime in the middle of the night, Chris sat sideways in that narrow hallway. It was the only place in the room he could brace his back against one wall and the butt of the loaded shotgun against the other. Then he put the muzzle of the shotgun in his mouth. It must have had that sour, tangy cold taste of metal. He was tall and had long arms, so he was able to push the trigger with his thumb. The gun was inexpensive, and when they found him the next morning, the wooden stock had cracked in firing.

Because his room was at the end of a long, otherwise vacant hallway, nobody heard the sound and his body wasn't found until morning. The motel manager called the police, who notified Dianne. There was no note, an odd omission. The autopsy report showed no trace of drugs or alcohol. He had been cold-sober and wide awake, with no apparent wish to say goodbye or to explain himself in any way.

My father, in Missouri, called me in Connecticut and my middle brother Dave, now the oldest, in Pennsylvania. It was assumed that I would deal with my mother in D.C. She had lived there since the divorce, while my father had remarried and moved away. At seventy-six, my mother's memory was failing, although she still managed on her own in her small apartment. I knew I had to tell her in person, but I wasn't sure how she would react or whether she would be up to traveling to Nevada for the funeral.

I didn't want to tell her about Chris the same way my father had told me. On an unremarkable Saturday morning, I had been in the upstairs bedroom of my house when the phone rang, and I had answered it without a thought. I was surprised to hear my father's voice; he usually called on a Sunday afternoon. He told me without preamble that Chris had shot himself and was dead. I sat down on the bed abruptly, as though I'd been pushed. I dimly remember screaming and then crying, and not being able to stop. The phone was still in my hand and I could hear that his voice was droning on. I managed to say, "I'll call you back." When I called him back half an hour later, everything was in place again, the wound sutured over. My crying had stopped. Not that I had stopped it, it just went away somewhere. We discussed travel plans and hotel reservations. Hovering above this strange conversation, like a floating figure in a Chagal painting, was my brother.

As I moved through the train station to make the trip to D.C. to tell my mother, everyone's voice sounded tinny. Unable to read my book, I stared out the window. Once at my mother's apartment, I found that I understood my father's dilemma: there is no way to lead up to this kind of news. Within a few minutes of my arrival, I just told her that Chris had died. She seemed to take it in, then asked, "Did he kill himself?" She seemed mostly curious about that one thing. To spare her, I had decided to hold that part back, but when she asked this uncanny question I realized I was actually sparing myself. It was too much for me, but somehow, she knew. I avoided a straight answer, saying instead, "We don't know the cause of death yet."

She cried, briefly, then stopped. She said she wanted to go to the funeral.

I helped her decide what to pack, what to discard from the fridge. At the front desk she told them to hold her mail. At the airport she asked me again how he died, if we knew the cause of death yet. And then again later, when the plane touched down. I was jolted both times, but stuck to the non-answer until we actually arrived at the house in Carson City, where Dianne and the kids were. As I was getting Mom settled in the guest room, she asked me again.

"You were right," I said. "He did kill himself. That's how he died."

"How?" she asked, just gathering the facts.

"He shot himself." I wondered if it was a mean way to say it, so bluntly like that. He died of a gunshot wound to the head? Does that soften it? She paused, but only for a few moments.

"At least he was decisive," she said. That was all. A cop told me the same thing a few weeks later, that this is the least ambivalent way to commit suicide. It is not a cry for help.

I woke up on the day of the funeral in a state of exhaustion and intense anxiety. My whole body wasn't just on edge, this was the *full red alert, man your battle stations*. I felt unfamiliar with myself. I could almost feel my brain frantically reorganizing, trying to make a space large enough to receive this new event. This act of my brother's was like a boomerang, a shuddering backward surge of destructive power, a whiplash event that undid all that had come before.

This violent act of my mild-mannered brother threw everything back into question, reopened every closed door. Remember that Thomas Wolfe book, *You Can't Go Home Again*? I think it should actually be, *You Can't Leave Home, Ever*. Because this wasn't just about his depression, or his job, or even his wife and kids. It was about all of us. But what my father had not said, what I had not asked, what my mother had not asked, was the question everyone asks about a suicide: Why?

It had occupied my entire mind from the time I had hung up the phone with my father. For anyone on the receiving end of a suicide, especially a violent one, it's the inescapable question. The death is there, but the *why* blunts the impact for a while. It's the leaf on every tree, the word in every mouth, every story in every newspaper.

Because I couldn't think about Chris's suicide for long, I focused on how we would manage the funeral and its aftermath. When my brothers and I were children, my father came up with an ingenious plan: he showed us a silver dollar and explained very solemnly that it was a "peace medal" and that whoever fought the least, or diplomatically persuaded the others not to fight, would win the medal for the following week. I was the only one who ever won it, and I slept with it under my pillow week after week for a few months until he retired it for lack of competition. In any situation involving the family, my natural inclination was to anticipate all the things that could possibly go wrong and try to prevent them. On this day, my mother was one of those things that could go wrong.

Nowadays, she seemed like a sweet little old lady. With her wispy white hair, tentative shy smile and soft voice, she was apparently harmless. But she could still gather her will, pull the bow taut and release an arrow, without ever opening her eyes or seeing that she had hit her target. The most dramatic time she had done that was when she decided to divorce my father, shortly before their thirty-year anniversary.

The visible tip of their marital iceberg was his mostly benevolent dictatorship, and her passive evasion and resistance. He was the irresistible force, she the immovable object. Their power struggle was expressed not in loud arguments, or even angry words, but in a fault line running through every sentence and every reply, every dinner table conversation, every decision made. Still, none of us saw it coming when, without warning, she simply had the locks changed one day while my father was at work. When he came home to their Washington, D.C. apartment near Rock Creek Park, she refused to let him in, or even to talk to him through the door. He stood there in the hallway, dumbfounded, for a long time before walking away.

She was right that he tried to control her, but it hadn't started out that way. She had married a sweet, awkward young man who fell in love with her because she was so smart, so kind and patient. He imagined the perfect family, so different from his own: they would have three children and live happily ever after. He even named their first child Christopher Robin, after the children's book—how sweet, people thought, not registering the undercurrent of impossible expectation.

After she got sick the first time, a couple of years into the marriage, he was completely out of his depth, with no one to advise him. After the next episode, the one Chris had written about, there were by then three children to look after, and he fell into his doctor role, making all the decisions and trying to manage her life, and also pretending everything was perfectly normal and unremarkable. Where was the help for him? It was 1950—no respectable family would admit to having a mentally ill member.

When I visited her some months after this separation, I sensed that in her mind, he was still there—just out in the hallway, waiting for her to make up her mind about what she wanted. She knew that she had locked him out, but never seemed to register that he would take that as a rejection, that he would, in the year afterwards, move toward an actual divorce. She seemed not to put the pieces together. For her, the marriage was on hold while she was mulling over how it felt to live without his oversight. She only reluctantly signed the divorce papers when Dave and I pressured her a year later, out of pity for our father. He had been rendered powerless in the face of her decision to lock him out, and equally powerless in the face of her curious indifference to finishing what she had started. She finally signed the papers, saying she still wasn't sure about it.

After the divorce, she made a small, manageable life for herself and asked me occasionally how my father was doing. She had a kind of nostalgic fondness for him, as though he was an old friend she'd lost touch with. My father remarried, but confided to me that he never would have chosen to leave my mother, that he still worried about her.

The day of the funeral, late summer in Nevada, was mercilessly hot and flat. Some of us had been to the funeral home in the morning and were exhausted already. Around noon, we all changed from our wilted clothes into black suits and dresses. Heather was with a neighbor. Chuck complained over and over about his uncomfortable new suit, his first ever, but he got no response from his mother. Dianne's eyes were completely expressionless, fixed somewhere out on the horizon. There wasn't anything left to her.

The funeral home had sent a limousine to the house, and the four of us rode silently to the hotel where my father and his wife waited outside. They got in, sitting as far away as possible. My father directed a firm *hello* toward us, then turned away resolutely—there would be no further conversation.

There were no hugs, there was no crying together. We were each floating in a bubble of private shock. Walking into the funeral home, I delayed a bit so that my father would be far ahead of us. My mother, though, tried to catch up to him, clearly wanting to say something. I managed to get between them and cut off her access.

Why? Because any normal reaction to the reality of where we were and what we were doing would have been against the rules. We had been given the message so many times, growing up: Do not react to things that are upsetting, or overwhelming, or even catastrophic. We had not shown any reaction when Mother went downtown in her nightgown and was brought back by the police. Nor when she acted so bizarre in the stationery store that she went back to the hospital for the third time, had more ECT, and didn't recognize us when we went to visit. We appeared not to notice that every afternoon when she drove to pick us up after school, the fifteen-mile-an-hour crawl of the Oldsmobile meant that she had started drinking around noon.

My brother Dave was sometimes the whistle blower when we were kids, and he paid the price. We always had dinner together, proving that we were a normal and functional family. But this one time, David, just turned fourteen, dared to notice and comment on our mother's semi-incoherent, paranoid, alcohol-fueled ramblings. My father backhanded him, then lifted him bodily out of his chair, and hit him again as he fell sideways onto the floor. After a few more punches, he dragged him across the living room into his bedroom and slammed the door, leaving a frozen silence as the rest of us sat stunned, forks in our hands. My father sat down at the dinner table, breathing hard, looked around and said, "What were we talking about when we were so rudely interrupted?" My mother, looking straight ahead, started to eat the bite of food she had been holding in mid-air. Chris was lost in his own world; we didn't even exchange a glance. I took a few more bites, too, and let five minutes pass before asking to be excused, so that god forbid it wouldn't look like a comment on the insanity that had just transpired and then been silently and forcefully disavowed. I had learned the lesson: We do not acknowledge what we cannot face.

Once the funeral was underway, and the minister was beginning the eulogy, I wondered if he would say it was suicide, not just the untimely death of this forty-six-year-old husband and father. He did. But as he started going off on a religious tangent, my mind began to wander.

I thought of Chris, lying in the closed coffin with what was left of his head wrapped in about thirty layers of gauze. I had insisted that those of us who wanted to could see him one last time, on the morning of the funeral. The director had hung back discretely while we filed into a side room to Chris's open casket. I recognized my brother by his hands folded on his chest, even though when I touched them they were stone-cold and stone-hard. I wouldn't have said I knew his hands all that well, but it turns out I did. I remembered them from when he held the *Cowboy Bob* book and read to me. Chuck and I stood close beside Chris, looking down at his body. Chuck was carrying a folded note, slipped it in quickly, and pulled his hand back out of the coffin. I took his hand again as he reached out for mine, both of us trembling and cold.

Eventually, after the funeral, the burial, the church reception, we all went back to the house. Despite the heat, someone suggested sitting on the back porch to talk and I signaled that I would get Mother out of the way. I took her back into her room on the other side of the house; by then she was tired, confused, and disoriented. She agreed to take a nap, lying down on top of the faded chenille bedspread, curled on her side with a little pillow, looking both childlike and old. I was relieved, thinking I wouldn't need to worry about her for a while.

Half an hour later, as the rest of us were talking about the funeral, and what Dianne and the kids would do now, I looked up and saw a tiny white-haired figure blinking groggily in the bright sunlight, just outside the back door. It was Mother. She got her bearings and started in my father's direction, walking across the dry grass, shading her eyes with her hand. I saw the way she held her head up high, focused on him, staring at him, willing him to stay where he was. She, whose hesitant, tentative walk had maddened me with impatience a thousand times, was moving with force and determination. She, the embodiment of ambiguity and passivity, had come to one of her rare and unequivocal conclusions and was going to declare it. He was no match for her, he with his authoritative voice and his implacable logic, his imposing height and his stiff, bristle-brush hair. In the most important things, he never had been.

Everyone stopped talking. I knocked my plastic chair over backwards as I jumped up to intercept her. Because she was physically frail and half-blinded by the sun, I was able to steer her back into the house. Turning her away from her target, I frantically willed her to become the little old lady she had been just half an hour before. Soon enough she lost focus and became that little old lady, harmless and forgetful; even her walk changed. Holding her arm, I could feel her slow down as she reclaimed her timidity. When I came back to the porch later, my father and stepmother had left. The next morning, when I drove them to the airport, none of us mentioned my mother.

As a family, we treated my brother's death as just another event to get through and move on from. But his suicide was like a depth charge, first dropping quietly below the surface, then exploding, its sound muffled deep underwater. Afterwards, the debris floated to the surface. It could have been coincidence, but within months, my mother's forgetfulness forced her into a nursing home; shortly thereafter my father was diagnosed with cancer. Dave retreated into his own world, rarely responding to my infrequent letters or calls.

This account began as a kind of confession of my guilt at preventing my parents from having something that was rightfully theirs. As it turned out, the day of Chris's funeral was in fact their last chance to speak. I've faulted myself for blindly following the rules I had learned long ago, doing what I had blamed my parents for doing: simply disavowing the reality in front of us, and forcing silence where there should be acknowledgement. And yet I couldn't remember making any decision; I had simply acted. Why?

In revisiting that moment, I am back there in the plastic porch chair, leaning into the conversation, suddenly seeing my mother standing in the sun. I see her pushing open the door, and I see her walking, and now I remember knowing instantly that nothing good was going to come of it.

She would have blamed him for something, and it probably would have had some truth in it; she was not a stupid woman. It wouldn't have been anything that brought them together even for a moment—like "Where did we go wrong?" It would have been a whiplash of accusation: "This is your fault." And he wouldn't have said anything at all, because the hot, dry Nevada air would have buzzed with

the memory of her insanity, her shock therapy, her hospi-
talizations, all of the arrows of blame aimed squarely at her.

There would have been no epiphany, no new insight, no
forgiveness for mistakes made, perhaps not even a tear shed
for my brother. My instincts were right, then: stopping her
at that moment protected us all. Not by denying what had
happened, but by accepting it.

The last "why" has lingered for years, too. Chris ended
his life with no explanation, no apology, and no blame. He
is not going to come back and tell us, "This is why I did it."
If he had written a note, we would have ignored everything
he left out. If we'd had one reason to latch onto, we could
have pretended it wasn't all those other things we were afraid

it was. If we are ever going to hear him, then we just have to hear his silence, in which all whys are possible and none of them, in the end, matter.

mɯ

A PILGRIM UNAWARES

Linda Parsons

Live always at the 'edge of mystery'—the boundary of the unknown. —J. Robert Oppenheimer

DOORS, GATES, WINDOWS. We never know which to open and slip through, which might bring the best sun and possibility—or shadow. We simply must choose and leap. I made such a leap last year in applying to the poetry workshop, "O Taste and See: Writing the Senses in Deep France," led by Dr. Marilyn Kallet, creative writing professor at the University of Tennessee. After a sudden life change in 2014, I needed this trip. I needed to take flight, both literally and figuratively, to affirm I could blossom in the world on my own. I had spent a year gathering my wits and strength, refocusing, no longer on two but on one with such newness—of time, of projects, of dreams, of taking leap after leap. But newness comes with its own baggage—solo international flights, leaving my elderly companion (my sheltie), melding with other poets, writing a poem a day. Fear, at least unease, turned to empowerment as I found my gates and sailed through O'Hare and Frankfurt, to be met at the Toulouse airport and driven past the brilliant mustard fields along the way to the village of Auvillar.

I'd traveled overseas before, to the UK and Ireland, but the Ireland trip was sixteen years ago, before the high security imposed after 9/11. When those on the tour bus learned my then-husband and I were poets, they clamored for Irish poems. In the heady pace of stop after stop, there would be no poems about emerald Eire, her thick cream and soda bread, fuchsia dense as the laurel hills of the Great Smoky Mountains. But my reluctance was more than exhaustion and overstimulation. The source of my work is *home*—what I've lost in past homes and gained in new ones, its slippery ideal, its many wounds, joys, shades of gray. No matter where I roam, the lifeblood of my work is rooted in family and Tennessee. Even more than concerns of traveling alone, I worried how I might integrate my heartwork into the French environs and experience, if at all.

Auvillar was heaven to me as a gardener: the trellised roses, stonecrop sprouting from terracotta roofs, calla lilies big as saucers, hidden courtyards reminiscent of Charleston's best. Running my hands along scrolled grillwork, half-timbered houses, and monastic frescos, sometimes stumbling on cobbles on my way to the day's poetry workshop, it seemed time had stopped in this Gallo-Roman village. Every morning we gathered for our workshop in Le Cebo studio at Moulin à Nef, the renovated country house of studios and living quarters for artists in residency. Our initial assignment was to write an ode from our outing the day before to the Valence d'Agen market, just as Pablo Neruda, the Chilean poet, wrote daily odes—to his socks, an orange, his plate, an onion. The market held so many possibilities—vegetables like jewels, fruits and fish as if just plucked from the tree or sea, rabbit-eared Sarmentine loaves, dusky men smoking in café doorways. But it's important for my work to be *from*, not *about*, to reach a depth rooted in my own experience and introspection. I needn't have worried, for the irony of a shop sign, "The Secrets of Pain" (bread), unlocked the first of five poems weaving my experience of a broken marriage with the gardens, narrow streets, and river of Auvillar (the Garonne). Whether triggered by the beauty and richness of the place, its history and food (le canard! pain au chocolat!)—or my own growth as a poet alone for the first time—a breakthrough happened that week in France, the breakthrough of *being* in two places—a joining of my own poetic intentions with my physical surroundings. Fully home, while not home.

I had read a bit about Auvillar's history before leaving home but was largely consumed with the many details of preparing for my first international trip alone. I had not grasped the significance of the village being on the annual pilgrimage route to Santiago de Compostela (field of stars, or the Milky Way), also called the Way of St. James. Pilgrims from many countries, hikers or backpackers to my eyes, passed daily through town, often with staffs or metal walking poles. They take up this route as a spiritual path or retreat for their spiritual growth, walking through France to the shrine of the apostle St. James in the Cathedral of Santiago de Compostela in Galicia, Spain, where tradition says the saint's remains are buried. On my own daily walk to hear and create poetry, I had noticed the small figures high on buildings around the village, appearing like the Miller and the Friar from *The Canterbury Tales*, and the symbolic scallop shells embedded as keystones over doorways as guideposts for the walkers.

Now home and reading more about the yearly journey, it all makes sense. Pilgrims have walked this route since the Middle Ages, smack through the village of Auvillar, which honors and welcomes their centuries-old pilgrimage along the same road, or camino, I walked with my sister poets. My trip, I have realized, was far more than the wonders I devoured with all of my senses, even more than the hoped-for breakthrough in my being and writing. Again on native soil, I can say that the Tennessee River is alive and flowing in the Garonne, that my own violet spiderwort in Knoxville swayed among the violettes of Auvillar. Yes, sometimes you must leap into the unknown—the vast, black Atlantic beneath you for hours, the chockablock security line in Munich nearly making you miss your flight. You must stray from home alone, set out on your personal pilgrimage even if the way is unlit and long, for you will return with a full cup and heart, despite sudden turbulence. In the village, the mourning doves called not just in the early morning and at dusk, but all day and into the night. They cooed *Don't leave…us, don't leave…us,* or so it seemed. I doubt I can ever fully leave Auvillar. My photos remind me of the bright teal shutters and royal blue doors, the grapevines latticed on bamboo, the meals et vin, oh the meals et vin. My poems written there spade ever deeper into home ground, the wellspring of my true work. Whether or not I return to Deep France, I am learning to embrace the pilgrim within, unaware of my leaden pack or the sky turning gray, realizing at last that the road I have chosen has actually chosen me.

[Ed. note: Read Parsons's poem on page 241.]

*L*inda Parsons is an editor at the University of Tennessee in Knoxville. She served as poetry editor of *Now & Then* magazine for many years and wrote a column, "The Writing Well," for *New Millennium Writings* for five years. Her poems have appeared in such journals as *The Georgia Review, Iowa Review, Prairie Schooner, Southern Poetry Review, Shenandoah,* in Ted Kooser's syndicated column, *American Life in Poetry,* and in numerous anthologies. Her fourth poetry collection, *This Shaky Earth,* was recently published by Texas Review Press. Parsons's adaptation, *Macbeth Is the New Black,* co-written with Jayne Morgan, was produced at Western Carolina University, and her play, *Under the Esso Moon,* was read as part of the Tennessee Stage Company's New Play Festival, both in early 2016.

Contact Marilyn Kallet at mkallet@utk.edu for details on the poetry workshop in Auvillar, France, normally held in mid-May each year. The Virginia Center for the Creative Arts (VCCA) in Amherst, Virginia, sponsors the workshop and other artist residencies, with Cheryl Fortier as the resident director of VCCA France in Auvillar. Visit the VCCA site at *www.vcca.com.*

NATURAL REFLECTION

An Interview with *NMW* Founder,
and Inspired Raconteur, Don Williams

By Brent A. Carr

THIS INTERVIEW TOOK PLACE OVER *several days in the original head-quarters of New Millennium Writings, where its founder still lives with his wife, Jeanne. Graced by woods and hills and singing streams, and a flag depicting the Whole Earth, it's a fitting setting for one who has made a career of looking to a future worth having.*

BAC: *Tell me how New Millennium Writings came to be.*

DW: I launched it in 1995, motivated by one part each inspiration, despair, fear, ambition, and a vow I'd made to myself ten years earlier.

BAC: *What was that?*

DW: I'd gotten a job at *The Knoxville News-Sentinel*, a mid-size, Top 100 paper I was thrilled to be working for. It was a destination paper for folks in the region, because East Tennessee's a beautiful place, and the paper was both profitable and unionized, meaning decent benefits and starting salary awaited.

Still, getting that call from the paper in the middle of 1985, asking me to come in for an interview, represented a dilemma in a way, because I had ambitions of bigger things, bigger towns, but they butted up against a lot of reasons to stay in the region. My wife Jeanne had an inspiring career going in a special ed program at a large public school. I had strong family ties that included people who were doing amazing things, but three of my siblings were in Nashville, and our mother was recently widowed, so as the closest child I felt a need to be there for her, for at least a couple of years. Plus, I had ideas about some books I'd like to write based on amazing things that'd happened in the region.

I'd won decent journalism awards at my previous job, a small paper where I'd done it all. I'd been an investigative reporter, feature writer, columnist, copy editor, and headline writer, so when the *Sentinel* called, I was in a position to write myself a pretty good ticket.

As I say, I was excited, until about my third day on the job. And that's when I realized there was something rotten in the state of Denmark...

What was that?

I got this impression that half the people there were walking around with a knife in their backs. I say half because there were, and still are, good folks at the paper—but in August 1985, it seemed damned near *everybody* was a target of cliques, gossip, harsh criticism—and it made me realize why I'd never much liked being where lots of people are packed into a small space day after day. You probably know the sort of infighting I'm talking about. College professors complain about it.

Newspapers were even worse because you had so many egos—half of them drunk on a half-pint of fame...or whatever—concentrated into a few hundred square feet and competing for shrinking *inches* in a newspaper where nobody's getting rich. It's like the old joke about college faculties: Why is the infighting so fierce? Because the stakes are *so low*.

It's the same at papers.

I felt like I'd entered a novel by the late Ken Kesey, a writer I'd visited in Eugene, Oregon long ago, and corresponded with over the years. He wrote at least two novels that involved that old Jungian notion of scapegoats—*One Flew Over the Cuckoo's Nest* and *Sometimes A Great Notion*. Of course, those books are so cosmic that anything you say about them is reductive—but both are at least in part about the compulsion to stone anyone who stands out.

Anyhow, about August 11, 1985, standing in the hallway outside my little office—which I shared with five others—I made a vow that come hell or high water I'd be out of there within ten years. Of course, I aimed to leave a lot sooner than that.

Why didn't you?

Lots of reasons. Jeanne was having babies, and both our careers were going well.

Within a year, I was making half my own assignments and writing a weekly general interest column. I got on a roll, real fast, and started winning awards and so I got to realize a lot of dreams.

I'd always been a space buff, and on the twentieth anniversary of the first moon landing I got to interview ten of the twelve who walked on the moon, all for a series of articles that went national. And I spent several days training as an astronaut, including deep water weightlessness and operating all sorts of gizmos.

And I hiked all over the Great Smoky Mountains, including portions of the Appalachian Trail, and wrote it up. I interviewed all kinds of celebrities—gurus like Ram Dass and Robert Bly, musicians like Leon Russell and Charlie Daniels and Dolly Parton—I once sang backup for Dolly, who was giving an impromptu concert for a fan in a convalescent home—but that's another story.

And I interviewed presidential candidates and artists and lots of writers. I made it a point to interview every major author who came through, and there were lots of them. People like

*Don's photo of Ken Kesey on his Oregon farm in November 1979.

John Updike and William Kennedy and Nikki Giovanni and Lee Smith and George Plimpton, the "participatory journalist" who founded the *Paris Review*. He'd play one series of downs as NFL quarterback, or get in the ring with a world class boxer *to see what that was like*. Just crazy stuff.

I just explored every subject that interested me, from particle physics to schizophrenia, to living on the streets, to the region's amazing history. Crazy interesting people hail from here. Dolly, Davy Crockett, Sam Houston, and Sequoyah, a distant relation who invented the Cherokee alphabet. Hank Williams's last night alive was in Knoxville. The Everly Brothers, whose harmonies influenced the Beatles, once lived here, and a hundred other well-known country artists. Save for the Million Dollar Fire in 1897, Knoxville might've become Nashville, or something like it.

And I covered every kind of human drama. Did a six-part series about writer Libba Moore Gray's courageous battle with breast cancer, at her request. Must've written 10,000 words for that. Because I was winning awards and adding readers, I was allowed to *write long*, and I made the most of it. I loved the New Journalists: Tom Wolfe, Hunter Thompson, Truman Capote. Not to make false comparisons, but I sought to become a stylist like them—unheard of in those days for a midsize newspaper.

Long and short of it was, I got paid *to have fun*. Took rides in glider planes and hot air balloons, and bungee-jumped and went whitewater rafting and skied and shot skeet. I'd go spelunking in incredible caves and get paid for it. Tried my hand at a pre-life regression, hypnosis, and other New Age stuff. Took adventurous vacations. Swam with dolphins and manatees and wrote it up. On and on. Concerts by musical heroes—The Moody Blues, Joan Baez, Bob Dylan, Crosby, Stills and Nash—and wrote those up.

How could you ask for a better job?

So why did you quit?

It's complicated. As you know, Tennessee's a very red state. My vote for president has seldom if ever counted—thanks to the

Electoral College. I'm a science-based progressive. And while I was born too late to be a hippie—just missed it—I was inspired by many of their ideas, along with the Beats and psychedelic poets and rockers, and peaceniks and visionaries.

When the first Gulf War came on, 1990, I was opposed at a time when the paper's editor was pro-military. And so I wrote several articles against the war and against global warming—heresy in a coal-producing state like ours. I think that's about the time opponents of my column began to form a line. I'd never really gone political before.

How did you become such a rebel?

Good question. My sister Rebecca reminded me just yesterday that we hail from a family of people who *do the unexpected.* My father grew up in a coal mining town, and that seemed to be his destiny, but then World War II came along and he went to Europe, fought in the Battle of the Bulge under Patton, and so on. He packed along his guitar and won some contests. Wound up performing in a USO-type show, called "Glory Road," by and for soldiers. There came the moment in every show when soldiers are sitting round a fake campfire and a brother in arms says, "Play us a song, Jim," and my Dad, who was also named Don Williams, would pick up his guitar and croon that great old song, "When My Blue Moon Turns to Gold Again."

When Dad came home he wound up in a well-known gospel duo named Don and Earl, and they performed live across the country, on more than thirty radio stations—including some high-powered border blasters in Mexico.

We'd get letters—and orders for songbooks and records—from as far away as England and the Canary Islands.

My mother is a nature lover and artist, who darn near swoons at the sight of a rainbow or say, a luna moth, and would take us to explore clear running creeks or on walks through the forest. She and Dad were both readers, and books were all over the house.

My sisters are both nature lovers. Rebecca is an amazing floral designer and her gardens are a wonder. Kathleen founded the Tenn Green movement through her Tennessee Parks and Greenways Foundation, and has worked wonders saving awesome waterfalls and much else from development. My brother Rod, a Vietnam vet, served as a Nashville metro-councilman and is now a popular blogger known as "A Disgruntled Republican." My brother Tim, also a Republican, got richer than God in the banking and finance industry.

My family tends to swing for the fences, so to speak, so it surprises friends to learn we were raised in a fundamentalist household, here where the Bible Belt latches onto the Republican Party.

When did you get an inkling that you could be a writer?

In the fourth grade, a teacher named Mrs. Rogers grabbed me by the shoulder as I was running out to play baseball, and told me she thought I could be a writer one day. I had written a poem about the Alamo, based on a song by Marty Robbins. The only words I still remember are...

One hundred and eighty men died brave/ And now they have deserving words upon their grave.

(Laughs) That was before I realized the battle was part of a land grab by Anglos intent on extending slavery into Texas. Poor Mrs. Rogers. I remember the day in 1963 when a knock came at our class door and Mrs. Reed leaned on the door frame and told us our president had been killed. We were having lunch, and Mrs. Rogers was sipping milk through a straw, and I remember how milk streamed from her nostrils as she lost her composure and ran from the room.

After that came the Beatles and hippies and demonstrations and Vietnam and space travel and more assassinations and Nixon's impeachment, and so much more that's kept my head spinning the rest of my life.

What books were formative?

Oh my God. How far back do you want me to go? Does *See Spot Run* ring a bell, from the old *Dick and Jane* series? Before that, fairy tales and the Bible, of course, but there was a book called *Chippy Chipmunk Takes A Vacation* that had pictures of the Painted Desert and redwoods that made me want to see the world. That was second grade. The next year, *The Cat in the Hat Comes Back,* by Dr. Seuss, just slew me.

One day in fourth grade I feigned a bellyache and stayed home from school, and Mama brought me *Tarzan of the Apes*, with its great opening line: "I had this story from one who had no business to tell it to me..." I was hooked, spent all day reading that book, thought it was a true story about this baby raised to adulthood by apes who had their own language.

I got hold of the next two sequels in paperback, and started ordering them through the mail from Ballantine Books. Ah, the delicious smell of print and glue from those paperbacks in their manila envelopes...

They're embarrassing to re-read. Africans are depicted as little more than missing links. Just awful. Still, they were packed with wonder and challenging notions, and I must've read thirty Burroughs books, about Tarzan and Venus and Mars and the Earth's Core.

In seventh grade I started reading Jules Verne and H.G. Wells. Wonderful books. I picked up a novel by Robert Heinlein called *Tunnel in the Sky* and was smitten. Notions of star travel, portals through space, time travel, mental telepathy. That hooked me on science fiction. Arthur Clarke, Bradbury, Asimov...

Me and some friends got together along about '68, and formed the Seymour Space Club. I think it maxed out at about six of us, who'd trade books and save up lunch money to go see movies that put us in outer space for a while. *Planet of the Apes, Barbarella,* starring a sexy young Jane Fonda, and *2001: A Space Odyssey,* which still blows my mind. *Star Trek*, of course, captivated us. And we'd get together and spend the night watching Apollo moonshots.

Apollo 8—still my favorite space flight—changed my life.

How so?

That first beautiful picture of *Earthrise* over the moon's horizon at Christmastime, 1968, which had been a year of war and riots and assassinations and Richard Nixon's election. Nothing ever seemed so amazing as Apollo 8. So what if it didn't land on the moon? Humans were traveling thousands of times farther than anyone in the history of the world. Forget Columbus. Forget Magellan.

Apollo 8 was fulfillment of prophecy, as if Jules Verne had channeled Wernher von Braun, leader of our space program. He was a former Nazi, but he was *our Nazi*. Never mind.

It still amazes me to think that nearly a century earlier, Jules Verne, a Frenchman, had written about a space capsule *launched from Florida, with three passengers*. Like Apollo 8, that capsule *never landed on the moon*, just orbited, returned to Earth, *splashed down*, and a ship *plucked it from the sea*. Just astonishing.

*Photo Credit: Marilyn Kallet

Wow! How do you explain that?

I can't. I mean lots of writers have been prophetic, but not with such precision. Ed Mitchell, who piloted Apollo 14 to the moon, once told me a long theory about how the universe is suffused at the particle level with something akin to consciousness, and that doorways to prophecy and telepathy and so forth sometimes open. It has something to do with quantum physics. I've experienced enough inexplicable coincidences—some call it *synchronicity*—to make me believe it.

Anyhow, Apollo 8 turned me into a newspaper nut. I'd run out every day and pick up *The News-Sentinel* and scour it beginning to end, looking for tidbits about space travel.

That was my first taste of journalism, and I became a fan of several columnists, Mike Royko, for instance, and I imagined seeing my own postage stamp-sized picture there one day.

As a high school sophomore, I began publishing a little newsletter for the Seymour Space Club. I called it *The Space Beacon*, and wrote it out long-hand on notebook paper—usually about four sheets' worth—making copies with carbon paper. I even drew a little cartoon strip. I think circulation topped out at six.

What did your parents make of all this?

They liked that I was reading and writing and making good grades. I think they worried about my solitary ways and certain notions I was picking up and expounding.

Such as?

Evolution, geological time, sexual mores...of aliens. (Laughs)

You've got to remember my father was a gospel singer who was around lots of preachers who believed the world was 5,000 years old, and we were descendants of Adam and Eve, literally, and that unless you were born again you would burn forever.

Sometimes I damn near felt those flames, and I would writhe around trying to escape the inescapable truth of them. It took a while, but thanks to science—as revealed in fiction—I did.

I remember walking around school one day thinking: *OH MY GOD, I'm going to hell, because…I don't believe in hell…*

There were preachers then who could make anyone with a vivid imagination *experience* hell, especially a child who had lust in his heart. I grew up next door to several attractive girls who liked to sunbathe in the back yard adjoining ours, and I'd experienced my share of lusting. One such preacher came to the little Baptist church I grew up attending and delivered a sermon he'd spent years perfecting, called "A Tour Through Hell." He was a blond, athletic man—looked like a surfer—and he walked his audience through a version of hell so graphic it made your hair curl. Oceans of lava washing you, beneath tongues of blue and red fire, the stench of sulfur, screams of sinners, on and on. Later he opened an attraction in Gatlinburg that offered guided tours through a version of hell that was so hokey it disabused me of the entire notion. I wrote a story about all this, called "A Tour Through Hell" for an anthology called *Low Explosions* that came out in 2006.

So, do you believe in God?

Short answer? Yes.

And the long answer?

Define God. (Laughs)

OK, how about "The God found in the Scriptures?"

Hmmm, my long answer usually ends the conversation, but, as a seeker, I've asked that question myself to a lot of smart people.

So here goes. If by God you mean Allah or Yahweh—God of the Old Testament—I have to say no. I've read the Bible all the way through twice. Once as a child during "family altars"—a little singing, praying, and scriptures before bedtime—and again as a youngster bent on making myself "well-read." I read much of it again for a course my wife teaches at church. Each reading pushed me farther from religion.

Why?

Because while the Bible is beautiful at times, it's largely a freak show. So much of it depicts God as an angry, jealous, all-powerful ego run amok, smiting most everything in sight, empowering his Chosen to commit genocide, at times, and, at one point, drowning virtually everyone, after which Noah repopulates the earth by copulating with his daughters, who get him drunk first, as I recall. Later, God promises to come back and finish the job. Then there's the whole crazy notion of hell, and of murdering your own son to save the world. I can't admire a father who would do that. So, I'm not a fan.

A friend used to say, "You worship Yahweh, I'll worship my way."

So what is your way?

I'm science-savvy with a strong dose of wide-eyed hippie thrown in. As Joseph Campbell used to say, quoting ancient Indian texts, "That which in the thunder inspires awe, refers to Divinity." I've experienced lots of divinity. I count my blessings daily. Literally, I write down five each day. As I once wrote in a column, "Luck runs out, blessings never do." At least that's been my experience, and as John Updike once told me, "When it comes to the existence of God, you have to consider the evidence of your own experience."

I admire the true teachings of Jesus and Buddha—the ones I suspect were real quotations, anyhow.

I admire Buddhist thought for its emphasis on emotional and mental discipline and transcendent awareness. I don't believe the religions established in their names have remained true to their message. I'm not a fan of a Final Judgement, or Cosmic Justice or Karma, in the formal sense, nor those who try to scare or bribe children into being good.

I believe such prophets or gurus were more akin to modern savants such as Kesey and, well, a number of the Beatles—maybe all of them—and Martin Luther King, Jr. and Joseph Campbell and Ram Dass and

*Don's photo of a giant marble zodiac in Ken Kesey's foyer.

others who had Mountaintop Experiences and brought back gifts for humanity. That doesn't mean the world is devoid of meaning. People who've had Mountaintop Experiences—that's a metaphor mostly—either through meditation, fasting, wandering in the desert, eating mushrooms, or watching the Whole Earth rise over the moon, often come back talking about the importance of Love and the Golden Rule, in the face of infinity.

I've had enough such experiences to know what the effects have been on me. They've probably kept me sane. They definitely led me to a kinder, more open-minded place. I realize this is not universal, that people have been known to indulge every sort of behavior under every sort of stimulus—especially alcohol—as well as stone-cold sober. Lots of Jihadists, fundamentalist Christians and others preach abstinence of every sort, and such folks have been known to commit or encourage terrible crimes.

You mentioned mushrooms. Do you see them as a tool of enlightenment?

Well I don't want to turn this into an ad for psychedelics, but we in this country have spread such ignorance about drugs that I'll risk an answer. We're a nation awash in opiates and crystal meth and alcohol and tobacco.

And we should differentiate. True psychedelics are actually rather benign, compared to those, and can be of great benefit. True, they're not for everyone. You hear tales of people who take trips and never completely come back. I've never known any, but you hear such things. So, decide for yourself. Still, as Sy Safransky, founder of *The Sun,* suggested in an interview this year, LSD has gotten a bad rap. He started that wonderful magazine following just such a Mountaintop Experience.

I'd take it a step farther and point out that as a matter of historical record, the most spectacular advances during the past half century have been helped along by psychedelics. It's an astonishing list.

Steven Jobs, who led the computer revolution, said taking LSD was the most important thing he ever did. Bill Gates acknowledged using it as well, in a *Playboy* interview.

James Watson and Francis Crick, who discovered the spiral structure of DNA, micro-dosed, apparently quite a lot, during their research.

John ("Jack") Whiteside Parsons, the inventor of the solid rocket booster, without which there would've been no space shuttle and, therefore, no Hubble Telescope—which has revolutionized our knowledge of the universe, likewise partook.

Kary Banks Mullis, the Nobel Prize-winning gene-sequencing pioneer, certainly rocked the world. He sped up the Genome Project by decades with techniques developed after or while experimenting with LSD.

Lucy, the Australopithecus, maybe the most important missing link ever, is named for "Lucy in the Sky with Diamonds," the Beatles song, so draw your own conclusions.

On the political front, there's considerable evidence that John F. Kennedy used LSD prior to sending us to the moon and standing up to a room full of generals and other advisors who were urging him to nuke Cuba and the Soviet Union. Later he made a landmark speech urging us to embrace the Russians for the love they have for their families. Then he initiated the Nuclear Test Ban Treaty of 1963. Remember, this happened at the historical moment that Kesey and Leary and Alpert (later known as Ram Dass) were spreading the news about psychedelics.

Claire Booth Luce, Stanley Kubrick, Cary Grant, Joni Mitchell, Dylan, and scores if not *thousands* of other artists, scientists, musicians, writers, publishers, and activists were indulging by then.

Certainly, Stewart Brand, who launched *The Whole Earth Catalog* and made an icon of Planet Earth—in part by pressuring NASA to take a picture of the Full Earth and releasing it to the world—was a member of Kesey's Merry Pranksters, who toured the country in a psychedelic bus *before anybody knew what a hippie was.* The picture of the Whole Earth is as ubiquitous now as the Crucifix, and to me

---

*Don's photo of the Merry Prankster Bus in 1979 when Kesey gave it shelter behind his Pleasant Hill, Oregon home.

it's a better symbol—as it includes all humanity—and suggests infinite worlds beyond.

So, yes, this sort of consciousness is a new and rightful "religion," if you will. It's our paradigm, or *gestalt*—a marriage of reason, wonder, and transcendental awareness. It dares to take a chance on reaching out to the light of reason and goodwill in others...the *love of love* so to speak.

And yes, its modern disciples—the hippies—almost certainly did save the world.

You really think so?

It's undeniable by any honest person who examines the evidence with an open mind.

Nixon didn't make peace with the Soviets and Chinese from the goodness of his heart. At least, not that alone. People were in the streets. He didn't set up the EPA or limit nukes based on his own fondness for peace, and clean air and water for all. People were in the streets. People who'd had Mountaintop Experiences firsthand or else answered calls from those who did. The Beatles, Kesey, Ram Dass, Carl Sagan, Terence McKenna, Tim Leary, Joni Mitchell, Bob Dylan, our latest Nobel laureate for literature, yes...and, I'd wager, in times past, Jesus the Nazarene, Siddhartha, and many others.

Wow, so how did such beliefs influence NMW?

So, *NMW* was an uneasy blend of a fascination with the Whole Earth, computer technology, space travel, the future—the New Millennium dontcha know—Mountaintop Experiences, old cultural heroes, and much else, all married to a love of brilliant writing.

Do you still partake of Mountaintop Experiences?

Don't we all? When a child spins round and round real fast, or rolls down a hillside, or skips or walks with eyes closed, or gobbles

*Don's sister, Kathleen (left), and wife, Jeanne, are startled by crashing waves on the beach at Kesey's coastal getaway.

down candy by the handful? What's he or she doing? Changing their state of mind, enlarging their frame of reference. When aging CEOs slug down a shot or three of Gentleman Jack, it's similar. When a woman throws her hands in the air and cries out to God in a rockin' church, it's similar.

What do you do?

I'm into long distance running, for one thing, although lately I've been applying that energy to rescuing my house, my rentals, my yard, my car, my truck, and so on. But in the past ten years I've probably averaged ten miles or so per week. Some years much more. I've completed three marathons since 2005, the last in 2014. I hope to run another, possibly in 2017.

I meditate as well. I've a little program I run through in the mornings—a small yoga set ending in a short meditation. For mine and Jeanne's 30th anniversary, in 2009, my sons, Travis Ladonuel and Justin Isaac, helped me lay a stone labyrinth in our side yard. It's the classical pattern, which predates Christ by at least 500 years and appears damned near all over the world. I'd say I've averaged walking Jeanne's labyrinth at least twice a week. It speaks to my soul.

It can be a journey back to the womb, the primal brain, the center of the earth, the heart of a rose or a black hole. No rules here. Our grandchildren race through it. I've watched Jeanne pray her way through it. I've seen friends tiptoe, dance, stagger, kiss and hug their way through it.

I've walked it nude a dozen times at least. It's a great way to wind down after a long run. And I've sat beside it under a full moon and felt I was observing the Andromeda Galaxy shining slantwise there.

So, there are any number of ways to tap transcendence. My still-fit honey, Jeanne, runs on a treadmill several miles every morning and measures progress by the number of people she prays for. She goes up every family tree of all her relations, then prays for the world, country by country in the news. I've been tempted to write "The Machine Breaks," about a woman whose treadmill breaks and, unable to run and pray for the world, she asks her husband to fix it. Finally, he breaks a wrench, gives up and turns in.

That night the stars begin to fall…

Do you ever use "spirited substances" to seek transcendence?

It's funny, but many of what once were vices have been validated as medicine. There's medical marijuana, and sometimes I indulge the herb. I love the way it dilates time and brings out the colors, the sounds, nuances in people's voices, especially if I lay off the alcohol.

Turns out my favorite beer—Sweetwater's India Pale Ale—is a health food. Hops are great antioxidants, anticarcinogens. And I'm rather a coffee addict—minimum six mugs a day—and that's been shown to reduce the risk of prostate cancer.

New clinical studies—as well as some that our government halted in the sixties—show that LSD as well as *shrooms* and other psychedelics are little short of miraculous in treating alcoholism, depression, PTSD, fear of dying, and, as you have personally discovered, cluster headaches. It's a crime how we've demonized them.

I agree. Our irresponsible drug laws violate basic human rights. As a "Clusterhead," this has become painfully obvious. What I meant was, do you still use them for Mountaintop Experiences?

Most years, along about Easter, usually on a coastal stretch of some South Carolina island, I'll partake of mushrooms as a sort of sacrament, possibly the kind that Christians once partook of.

Bread mold, or ergot, is a natural psychedelic, and wine is, well, wine.

There's an epistle in the New Testament in which Paul asks Christians not to drink up all the best wine during communion, but to save some for late arrivals at the feast. So, who knows what all they might've done in waking dreams, but I'm pretty sure communion once consisted of more than a thimble of wine and a crust.

Tell me about your first psychedelic experience?

One night late in 1972 I think it was, I took a four-way hit of
windowpane. I had no idea what I was in for. I remember picking
up a piece of paper that left color trails in the air. Later, closing
my eyes, I toured the cosmos—falling across interstellar space,
drawn by a distant star, filled with great longing and fear of failure,
only to soar on past in endless repeating orbits. Same yearning,
same flyby.

Later I blinked and became a drop of protoplasm or something, spiraling down a perfect helix. I don't think I even knew
what DNA was at the time. I closed my eyes again and *became*
the melody in the music we were playing—I think it was The
Moody Blues' *Seventh Sojourn,* with its stellar harmonies and
soundscapes. The next day my world was all changed.

The sounds of my parents talking were precious to me. My
father was getting dressed for a trip out of town and he looked
like a God or something, so shiny and upbeat and powerful.

I never matched that first experience. Of course, I did very little
compared to Kesey or the Grateful Dead and it's not something
I advocate for everyone. But the times I did indulge opened my
mind to the amazing universe—as well as the impossibility of

defining reality. It's a point I often make in my writings: Whatever you say about the world risks diminishing it.

You never see the whole picture. I have a dog who goes crazy with joy at times. She runs loops in the yard, jumps up and down, sends things crashing with her tail. Wouldn't you like to be such a creature for five seconds? What must it be like to experience such bliss? And she's a mammal like us in many respects.

I suspect we knew such bliss as children. I can remember at about age five running with my brother Tim round and round and through our house, then under construction, rubbing and patting our new burr haircuts in a kind of joy that I can neither account for nor recreate.

And that's an experience close to my heart.

Now consider consciousness and natural phenomena distinct from my experience.

Annie Dillard does this in *Pilgrim at Tinker Creek*, in which she invokes real creatures—many equipped with bellows and pumps and jets and valves and eye-wipers and scissors and camouflage and songs and switches and compasses and radar and sonar and a thousand sorts of eyes that see colors we can't even imagine, on and on.

After a while you have to decide whether there's something sacred about such seemingly infinite variety here on Earth, and then consider the billions of other worlds we now know exist.

Surely some patterns are common to such worlds. Take the helix or, its cousin, the spiral. It's in your DNA, it's in tiny grooves on the ball of your thumb, your baby's cowlick, the water circling down your bathtub drain, the magnificent Andromeda Galaxy. Our own Milky Way. It's everywhere.

To me, that's a sacred symbol.

How did your 1972 Mountaintop Experience affect your life?

It changed me overnight and forever. Gave me a hint of just how vast and wondrous the universe might be. No other experience I've had, before or after, has equaled it.

It made me realize that we exist at the intersection of untold progressions into infinity. What we think of as time, energy, light, size, speed, density, sacredness, heat, even sexuality, are scales or progressions reaching in all directions.

Poets and writers frequently express this.

"The world is charged with the grandeur of God," says Gerard Manley Hopkins, and gives us a thousand examples in sprung rhythm.

As another poet, a member of The Moody Blues, wrote, in un-sprung, rhyming couplets in the sixties:

> *This garden universe vibrates complete.*
> *Some may get a sound so sweet.*
> *Vibrations reach on up to become light,*
> *And then thru gamma, and out of sight.*
> *Between the eyes and ears there lie,*
> *The sounds of color and the light of a sigh.*
> *And to hear the sun, what a thing to believe.*
> *But it's all around if we could but perceive.*
> *To know ultra-violet, infra-red and X-rays,*
> *Beauty to find in so many ways.*
> *Two notes of the chord, that's our fluoroscope.*
> *But to reach the chord is our life's hope.*
> *And to name the chord is important to some.*
> *So they give it a word, and the word is OM.*

To me, Dylan Thomas's *force* "that through the green fuse drives the flower" is sacred, if deadly. Jobs said Death is Life's greatest creation, because it makes new forms possible.

So that's my long answer. I try to embrace the idea *behind* Annie Dillard's assertion—maybe others said it first—that "Every day is a God," in that each day is new and miraculous and full of divinity, if hailed with open eyes.

So what's wrong with organized religion?

Too often it's a reducing valve that closes the mind. For some people, maybe most, it's The Answer. And that's dangerous. Don't get me wrong. Many live good lives in the church, where they find fellowship, redemption, opportunities for culture and self-expression, charity, healing, a refuge from violence. Marx called it the opiate of the masses, but for many it's an alternative to *actual* opiates, now washing our country. For others, it's a network, a hand up the ladder. For a few at least, it's a way to experience transcendence—to confront the Big Questions.

So what's wrong with organized religion? (Laughs)

As you know, I attended a pretty progressive church near my house for some years. Each Sunday I jumped through hoops to rationalize why I was uttering beliefs from the Middle Ages and even earlier, during the Nicene Creed and so forth.

I finally lost interest in going after the American flag appeared behind the altar alongside the religious icons already there. It was during our invasion of Iraq, and to me it was such a betrayal of the teachings of Jesus, not to mention outright *idolatry*. I'd been outspoken against the war, and I couldn't be a party to an organization that seemed to endorse killing.

Too often the church betrays its ideals in service of people who pay lip service to religion. That's what made it possible for fundamentalists to elect a manifestly ungodly man like Trump, and before him, George W. Bush.

I think most religions subvert the teachings of their alleged founders, turning them into mystery cults in service to the power structure, while attributing miracles and sayings to them that I doubt they ever uttered.

Finally, they promote superstition at the expense of science. I don't see anyone rising from the dead. I don't see any pregnant virgins. I do see the effects of global warming and evolution and technology born of science. People who should know better deny climate change, and therefore lend support to forces on track to eliminate half the species on Earth by the end of the century.

It's as bad as Holocaust Denial, because we could turn the Whole Earth into a burnt-out cinder.

So is this all there is? No afterlife?

Should I wake up again, after death, in some kind of new consciousness or body, I doubt if I'll be any more surprised than when I woke up in *this* world. Anything's possible. There's solace there, reason for hope.

Of course, I won't be surprised if I *don't* wake up from such a sleep. As Cormac McCarthy wrote in *Suttree*, "How surely are the dead beyond death. Death is what the living carry with them. A state of dread, like some uncanny foretaste of a bitter memory. But the dead do not remember and nothingness is not a curse. Far from it."

How did you go from reading science fiction to Suttree?

As a reader, I branched out starting about 1968, when a classmate named Larry Drain changed my way of thinking, with just a sentence.

Larry wore thick glasses and always had his nose in a book, and the jocks harassed him mercilessly, until he became a standout baseball pitcher, but what I'm about to tell happened before that gratifying development.

There'd been demonstrations the night before, led by Martin Luther King, Jr., during which protestors had stopped traffic in some city, and we were talking about it the next day before French class, and I'm ashamed now to confess I blurted out, "They oughta just run over them."

Larry was sitting in a nearby chair, nose in a book, and without looking up, he said quietly, "That would be murder."

I sputtered, "But if they won't get out of the way…"

And he just repeated, "That would be murder."

And that shut me up. The rightness of what he said was clear. Curious, I looked down at what he was reading, and it was Kurt Vonnegut's *God Bless You, Mr. Rosewater.*

I crossed the courtyard and checked out Vonnegut books, one after another. *Cat's Cradle, Slaughterhouse Five...* and even though these were science-fiction, they were a bridge to mainstream fiction. But don't get me wrong. I still read science-fiction from time to time, and actually have published a considerable amount—maybe ten percent of the stories in *NMW*. In fact, there's a story in *NMW* Volume IV, Issue 1, called "The Memory Pool," by Quentin T. Laredo, a pen-name I used. And I've written a draft of a novel called *The Forever Formula*, which I hope to finish one day.

You once said you were "an accidental English major."

I'd gone to the University of Tennessee with the vague idea of becoming an astronaut, but it took about one class of physics to make me realize I was out of my depth. I might've gotten a science degree but I was struggling to make ends meet, putting myself through college, and I just didn't have the energy to work all the math puzzles required of the physical sciences. Meanwhile, I was drawn relentlessly to literature.

Keats, Shelley, Byron, Hemingway, Fitzgerald, Frost, Hopkins, Flannery O'Connor, Homer, and of course, Shakespeare. I had this wonderful professor, Dr. Allen Carroll, who could do the Cockney and high-English accents and bring those plays alive.

Meanwhile, I was withdrawn as ever, and stayed home reading a lot when not working or in school. Two of the most influential books were *Cuckoo's Nest,* mentioned earlier, and *The Catcher in the Rye,* by Salinger. His story, "For Esme—With Love and Squalor," struck a chord deep down, really put me in an English café on a rainy day.

Finally, after about six years of scraping through, dropping out to raise money, going part-time and so forth, I looked up one day and realized I could graduate in three months if I took two more lit classes, and so I did.

So what did you do with your new degree?

I like to say an English degree is wonderful because you can do so much with it: wait tables, drive a taxi, pump gas, roof houses...

I'd meant to go far away and write the great American novel. Instead I met Jeanne, we moved in together, and both took jobs teaching at the retro-named but quite progressive Blount County Center for the Handicapped.

In 1979, Jeanne became pregnant with Alexis and we made the decision to get married. As a sort of honeymoon, our wonderfully unconventional bosses, Annie Selwyn and John Richardson, allowed us to take six weeks off and see the country. It was on that trip—in a little yellow, hand-painted 1965 VW van named Jasmine—that we went to see Kesey in Eugene, Oregon. It was

an amazing journey full of adventures and synchronicity, and it was during this trip I decided to embrace my new identity as a father without letting it end my dreams of writing.

I went back to work at the center and wrote an article about our work there, and got that published, then I wrote some ad copy, and a travel booklet about the 1982 World's Fair in Knoxville, and several articles about a trip I made to the Soviet Union the same year. I went to help a blind friend get around while he underwent an eye treatment that only the Soviets had at the time.

This led to a job at *The Mountain Press* in Sevierville, which led to *The News-Sentinel*.

I always meant to get away, but the timing of deaths and births and promotions and other things conspired against me, sort of like James Stewart in *It's A Wonderful Life*, which Jeanne and I saw just last week.

Still, I've managed to see a good bit of the world. Summer Solstice at Stonehenge, in 2002. They took down the fences and an amazing assortment of hippies and New Agers and gypsies and pagans and scientists and artists and world travelers converged

---

*Don's photo of Jasmine, on her journey west, as she pauses at Mt. Rainier for rest.

and drummed and danced all night to usher in the longest day of the year.

I've been all over Paris and Moscow—Saint Basil Cathedral, Lenin's Tomb, toked up under the Kremlin Wall in '82. I've been lava-hopping and kayaking in Costa Rica. All over this country, and spent an academic year at Ann Arbor, an academic oasis amid the ruins of industrial Michigan.

That came while you were at the News-Sentinel, right?

That's right. In 1991, I applied for a sabbatical at the University of Michigan, for a year of paid leave studying anything I wanted. It was a wonderful award, started by the NEH a few years before. I wrote "the novel that ate my life" there. (Laughs). Still unpublished.

One stipulation of the grant was that I had to promise to return to my job for a year. So, ten months after leaving I found myself back in the same rut.

That's when I started really reaching out to other writers around town. I helped found the Knoxville Writers Guild, strengthened my friendship with Leslie Garrett, a novelist who'd banged around Europe with Knoxville's own Cormac McCarthy. I'd contacted him while writing probably the longest newspaper profile anyone had written on Cormac, up to that time.

Still, there came a time when I felt I was just repeating myself.

Why didn't you leave?

By now we had *three* children. We were both just smitten by them. We all had friends and schoolmates. We had close family, Jeanne's job was going well. I was active in the Guild.

Plus, it had become clear that journalism was a shrinking ocean. Lots of good journalists were out of work. Opportunities were drying up, and I wasn't a kid anymore. The other daily in our town had shut down.

I was tired of the infighting, the pettiness of so much that went on, conflicts between management and union. It just never let up. *The Sentinel* was threatening to begin drug-testing, and I had no intention of pissing in a cup.

Some quit, others were fired, there was talk of downsizing, and I'd missed my window of opportunity. I remember the sinking feeling I got when corporate in Cincinnati sent suits down to give us a lesson in the future of journalism. To hear them tell it, it was all going the way of *U.S.A. Today.*

I couldn't see myself writing short, tight *brights* about Knoxville's power elite. I wanted to extend my wings, rewrite my, by now, *two novels*, publish more stories, and much else.

The coming New Millennium kept speaking to me. Few were talking about it in 1995, but I knew it would be huge, you could feel the momentum growing, and I wanted to *be there* when it happened. I'd spent years contemplating the future and notions like the Age of Aquarius. Not that I believed in such an age in the literal sense.

But I did believe that given progress in science, prosperity, peace initiatives, communications, and more and more people seeing the value in Mountaintop Experiences, a better world could be built. We might turn the Earth into a virtual paradise.

I believed it was a great opportunity to launch a journal in the vein of *New World Writings* or *The Paris Review* or *Glimmer Train*. I was kicking it around with a friend one evening and came up with *New Millennium Writings.*

It had an apocalyptic feel to it.

This wouldn't be your typical journal. I would "make it new" in every way, with innovative typography, shadow boxes, photographs and illustrations, notes from authors, kick-ass interviews, all bound between four-color covers. No genre would be off-limits.

The only criterion would be *the writing must sing*. We'd start twice a year, then go quarterly, maybe even monthly someday, while printing other books and venturing into other media.

And so, in 1995, hopped up on such notions and coffee, I remembered the vow I'd made my third day on the job, that come hell or high water I'd leave *The News-Sentinel* within ten years.

And did you, literally?

I left on August 8, 1995, the tenth anniversary of the day I arrived. I collected a $10,000 retirement fund I'd grown over ten years, and the editor said he'd be pleased to pay a modest amount to continue running my column, which I would write freelance.

And that's when you started NMW?

That's right. Boy, was I naïve. Starting a literary journal is not the way to free up more time for serious writing.

Still, it was exciting. I recruited Marilyn Kallet as poetry editor, asked John Updike, whom I'd interviewed for the *Sentinel,* again for *Writer's Digest,* to be the subject of our first interview. Got local writers Allen Wier and Jon Manchip White and prize-winning journalist Fred Brown to serve as literary judges. I recruited space artist Mark Maxwell to draw full-page illustrations.

My friend Liz Petty, an English teacher, and my gifted daughter, Alexis, pitched in, helping to screen stories. I rented a PO box in Knoxville, and put out a call for submissions.

I'll never forget how my brother Rod and I stood in the marble temple of the Knoxville Post Office, at PO box 2463, looked at one another, took a breath, as I turned the key. It was such a feeling of déjà vu. Our father had often stood in the same hallway, wondering what the day's mail would bring. To our relief, the box was packed.

When people asked me what I was doing, I used to laugh and say I was "in Manuscript Management." I was always moving big stacks of envelopes—stories and essays—and little stacks of letter-sized envelopes—poetry, mostly—from place to place.

First issue came out in April 1996. A big U-Haul type truck backed into my yard and dropped them off in cartons. I was proud of that first issue, with its four-color cover featuring a storm-tossed sea we called "In the Beginning," by Helen Hightower, but financially I took a beating that first year.

Suddenly, I started seeing articles about literary journals dying off. Of course, they're always dying off, as new ones emerge, but these weren't just ragtag, shoestring operations with bland covers. These were old, influential magazines.

I began to think I'd walked off a cliff.

With a daughter entering college, and two boys in grade school, I took a deep breath and made a list of how to cut costs and increase revenues. I would eventually cut production to once per year, *forget going quarterly*, much less monthly. I raised contest fees, asked the University of Tennessee English Department for a contribution, solicited more ads, even took part-time work crewing a hot air balloon, then hung out my shingle and started teaching creative writing courses that I scared up myself at the Tennessee Valley Unitarian Church in Knoxville.

That turned out to be a big success, and a heck of a lot of fun. I loved teaching and kept that course going for years.

So, it was scary, but by the middle of the second year I knew we weren't going to starve. Later, I published a book of journalism that sold out, helped some other writers publish their books, and slowly began building more name recognition, so that by the end of 1999 I felt sure the journal would be OK over the long haul.

So how did the New Millennium live up to your expectations?

Well, it isn't the Age of Aquarius, at least so far.

It sort of got hijacked. Following the biggest party the world's ever seen, came the biggest buzzkill. In 2000, despite losing the popular vote, George W. Bush got handed the presidency by five Republican Supreme Court justices. It's so ironic that these advocates of States Rights voted to revoke Florida's right to keep counting the votes.

Al Gore seemed the perfect candidate for the New Millennium. He was committed to stopping global warming, likely would've prevented 9/11 by retaining the active services of people like Richard Clarke. He had plans to mount a satellite to track changes in climate patterns and generally inspire the world by showing us the Whole Earth every day. He seemed destined.

Did you feel crushed, like Hillary supporters feel now?

Even more so, I think. It was so close in the Electoral College. Had Gore carried his own state he would've won—but Tennessee's a red state. And while it's pretty clear more people set out to vote for Gore on Election Day, even in Florida, a lot were turned away by long lines, others by official letters telling them they'd been removed from voting rolls. In a way, the butterfly ballots and hanging chads were the least of the offenses committed in Florida, but so it goes. It was a sort of slow-motion coup. Then as now, the person who got the most votes was denied the presidency.

This used to be a bigger deal. In 1960, my parents voted for Nixon over Kennedy. After it became clear Kennedy would win in the Electoral College but the winner of the popular vote was still undecided, I remember my parents looking very worried. Both said they hoped Kennedy—whom they voted *against*—would go ahead and win the popular vote, as it would be a sad day in America if the will of the people were subverted, and we would be a divided country. It's hard to get past how casually the media reports the fact that in two of our past five elections, the Candidate Who Got More Votes, in absolute terms, was not allowed to serve. The system IS rigged, in this case for Trump, in 2000 for Bush.

Which was worse?

Well, I've said for some time that the real damage was done in 2000. Robbing Al Gore of his presidency led to so many catastrophes: 9/11, never-ending war, millions dead, Europe under siege, the rise of ISIS, secret energy deals, the end of some international treaties, disastrous effects of fossil fuels. On and on. The other thing that was damaging was the rise of neo-conservatism, and just outlandish patriotism and what I call the Political Correctness of the Right.

You couldn't speak out against the war without being accused of Not Supporting The Troops and having your name dragged through the mud and receiving death threats. I experienced all of that because I refused to pretend the invasion, bombing, and occupation of Afghanistan and Iraq was missionary work. I was relentlessly critical of what I called the Cheney-Bush administration, and it drove my editors to distraction.

Please tell me your resistance did some good, somewhere.

Well, my columns got good traction. They showed up lots of places. My inbox was brimming most Fridays for about ten years. Not only Scripps Howard papers and the *Sentinel's* site, but also *BuzzFlash, Antiwar.com, Reader Supported News, opednews.com,* on and on, carried the columns. Plus they got out to an email subscribion list in the thousands—many of them *NMW* readers. And they went to lots of Big Media in Washington and New York. Helen Thomas was a regular correspondent. I was a paid blogger for *Knoxville Voice,* and even appeared once in a live panel discussion on *Russia Today TV.*

It was funny. I didn't set out to be a political columnist. I used to write about rainbows and sunshine and family life and moon-walkers and such. While I always tried to be provocative, the occasional political piece was just part of the mix. Then came the Bush presidency and 9/11.

I remember lying awake that night with a sinking sensation in my stomach. *We're never going to hear the end of this...*

So, I opposed as much of the jingoism and hate-mongering as I could, and I'll put my columns up against anyone's when it comes to *prescience.* I predicted the war would spread, many thousands would die needlessly, sectarian violence would take over, refugees would flood borders and destabilize the world, and no WMDs to speak of would be found.

It was all such a waste.

I believed then that everyone who cared about the future had to speak out and leave nothing on the playing field. I did every-thing I could at a time I felt the future of the planet was on the line.

So, in retrospect, the year 2000, rather than marking this great turning point in human consciousness, robbed us of a generation of progress. A generation we could not afford to lose.

In other ways, however, the New Millennium began exceeding all expectations.

I'm relieved to hear it. How so?

Advances in human rights, women's rights, gay rights, the reform of marijuana laws, the discovery of thousands of planets, the advent of private space ventures, the election of a black president, healthcare reform, such as it is, new climate change initiatives, astonishing progress in genetics and digital technology and renewable energy, self-driving cars, and newfound savvy when it comes to health and medicine, and a dawning realization that the War in Iraq was a huge mistake. Of course, it was more than that, as I demonstrated. It was a war crime. Every time I see some refugee lying dead on a beach in Europe, I think, "Dick Cheney's gift to the world."

Still, violent crime and warfare have declined, despite increased media coverage. You can chart it on a graph.

Can you point to any of your writings that made a difference?

Maybe it's my ego, but I like to think I helped turn the tide against Cheney. Early in 2004, I wrote a two-part column that opened with a prediction that he'd never run for vice-president again, because too many conflicts of interest had been exposed. I documented about fourteen of them, including his activities in the first Gulf War, during which he steered military contracts to Halliburton; how he then moved into the private sector and became Halliburton's CEO, benefitting from those fat contracts.

Then, he was asked to head up a committee to choose a VP candidate for Bush 43, and chose himself. After Bush took over, Cheney used lies from bribed and tortured people—Google "Curveball, al-Libi, and Chalibi"—to plant stories in the media, and drum up a phony case to bomb the hell out of Iraq again, invade and occupy the country, while Cheney resumed steering fat contracts back to Halliburton. I mean, Trump's got nothing on Cheney when it comes to conflicts of interest. I listed a dozen or so others.

A day or so after my column ran, I got a call from a *Rocky Mountain News* reporter thanking me for including research he'd done into Cheney's cynical unmasking of spies who didn't toe the line. I returned the compliment and said yeah, but it's like spitting into the wind, isn't it? To my surprise, he said, not really, have you seen today's *Washington Post?* They followed *you.*

Chris Matthews mentioned it that night, as credits rolled—asking a panel of distinguished pundits if there was anything to the rumor Cheney might not stay on the ticket. They all smiled and smugly shook their heads. I've often wondered whether he might've dropped off the ticket had they done their homework and looked into the charges we'd made.

So, I started a short-lived rumor. Still, after that it was open season on Cheney. Bush stopped listening to Cheney as Iraq went from bad to worse in his second term, and distanced himself from the Neocons generally.

I can point to other columns. A leader of the greenways movement once told me a series of articles I did about historic creeks feeding the Tennessee River in Knoxville inspired the creation of several greenways along their banks. And I rallied hundreds of letters and emails supporting my sister Kathleen's amazing work to establish migration corridors and protect great natural wonders across our state.

Other columns helped fund wheelchairs for the physically challenged, brought attention to over-development and such as that.

One never knows.

Does a Trump presidency worry you?

Let me put it this way.

The Sword of Damocles hangs over our heads. Global warming is real. Putin and Trump are calling for expanding their nuclear arsenals. On the other hand, they've talked about cooperating. Worse things could happen than making peace with Russia. Which will it be?

History is full of such turning points. We were given a precious opportunity at the end of the Cold War. Reagan and Brezhnev almost seized the moment at Reykjavik. They were an eyelash away from cutting a deal that might've eliminated all nukes on Earth by now, but a lack of trust kept them from acting.

After the Cold War we might've opened our arms to Russia, welcomed them into NATO, and ushered in a new era of world peace. Instead, Bush 41 gave us the New World Order.

What was that?

Well, another phrase for it is Monopolar Hegemony, a diplomatic way of saying we now run the world, as opposed to Bipolar Hegemony—when the old Soviet Union and the U.S. ran the world.

As Kesey said in another context, it's the oldest game in the world. Nothing new about it. Person with the biggest stick—dare I say biggest hands…ahem—runs the joint. Trump seems the least enlightened person ever. As someone said about Nixon, perhaps unfairly, "He's the darkness reaching out for the darkness." And Trump found plenty of it.

What worries me most is our lack of introspection. We throw around terms like "American Exceptionalism" all too easily. I've felt for some time that we're on the brink of committing some great crimes again.

You've paid a price for your outspokenness.

In some ways. In 2006, my editors—who twice endorsed Bush/Cheney—took me to a restaurant and asked me to tone down my opinions against Bush and Cheney. When that didn't work, they informed me the column would be cut back to every other week. It was a deal I could refuse, mostly because I knew it was an attempt to muzzle me, and so I quit.

The pushback was heartening. Hundreds of emails and letters flooded the editors in support—I know because many of them copied me. The paper ran only a small percentage, but they still dominated the letters page in several issues.

Of course, my opponents pushed back hard. It's a strange dynamic. People you thought were friends suddenly couldn't be reached. Invitations were revoked. Still, lots of people came to my defense, and my column ran on the Internet for years.

Why did you quit writing it?

For the same reason I gave up my writing class and turned *NMW* over to Alexis. The timing was right and other voices were calling.

Did you have any doubts or regrets about that?

What? Naming Alexis the Editor? Not a one. She's imminently qualified. An Honors English major, a professional writer who's had a hand in the business since its founding. I think she's done and continues to do a wonderful job. And Brent, of course, you're added value. I'm in awe of the graphics, the outreach to the LGBT community, the beautifully designed emails and bookmarks and website and social media. I like your ideas for the future. Digital versions and book publishing and so forth.

I couldn't be happier.

Thank you, Don. So what voices were calling?

I'd begun researching the most amazing story I've been around—better than Apollo 8 in its way—and that's the story of the Smoky Mountain White Caps.

It's got it all. Thundering hooves and shootouts, white hoods and robes, hand signals and secret oaths, scandalous affairs and music and moonshine, morphine and laudanum, bribes and conspiracies, jailbreaks and hangings, detectives and spies, secret oaths and screaming headlines, fiercely fought elections and petition drives, outrageous sacrifice, close calls and coincidences that would be unbelievable in works of fiction...

I also plan to take a look at novels I abandoned a long time ago. I'd like to pull together a book of stories, poems, columns. I need a clone! Maybe later on in the New Millennium...(Laughs).

Despite all the darkness you've encountered, what inspires you most?

I'm surrounded by angels. They're everywhere. My wife is a teacher and healer. My children and their mates are just full of love and good will. My mother, my sisters and brothers and friends and family work overtime to care for and rescue people. During the recent devastating fires in Gatlinburg and in and around the Smoky Mountains, the community response was nigh unbelievable. Just so inspiring.

Despite everything, I still see great good in most people I deal with daily.

They give me plenty of reasons to look forward to the future in this still-new millennium.

Award Winners
& Finalists

The editors and judges at

New Millennium Writings

are pleased to announce our

NEW MILLENNIUM NONFICTION AWARD

1ST PLACE
WRITING AWARDS XXXIX

Susan Nathiel

Middlefield, CT

Hearing Silence

1ST PLACE
WRITING AWARDS XL

Karen Hunt

Woodland Hills, CA

INTO THE WORLD

FINALISTS

XXXIX

Adrianne Aron, Berkeley, CA
Cathy Beres, Evanston, IL
David W. Berner, Forest Park, IL
Terence Cady, Santa Fe, NM
Kevin Camp, Washington, DC
Anne Frohna, Prescott, AZ
Myrna Greenfield, Brooklyn, NY
Richard Hague, Cincinnati, OH
Saffron Marchant, Hong Kong
Kate McCahill, Santa Fe, NM
Alberta Nassi, Sacramento, CA
Thomas Osborne, Atlanta, GA
Jesse Padilla, Normal, IL
Diana Perkins, Highlands Ranch, CO
Richelle Putnam, Meridian, MS
Christine Ritenis, Suffern, NY
Morgan Smith, Santa Fe, NM
Rachael Sokolowski, Truro, MA
Deborah Thompson, Fort Collins, CO
John Wagner, Montpelier, VT

XL

Hillary Adams-Maalouf, Minden, NV
Margo Barnes, Tucson, AZ
Sabrina Bess, New Rochelle, NY
Susan Bonetto, San Francisco, CA
Leeanne Carlson, Waller, TX
Cecilia D, Santa Clarita, CA
Rachel Fauth, Fort Salonga, NY
Linda Federico-O'Murchu, Montclair, NJ
John Gist, Silver City, NM
Evelyn Krieger, Sharon, MA
Jessica Kulynych, Simsbury, CT
Stan Mayer, Austin, TX
Jason Najum, Montreal, QC
Susan Narayan, Minneapolis, MN
Jean Noland, Coos Bay, OR
Gregory Ormson, Kailua Kona, HI
Darrin Pruitt, Brooklyn, NY
Catherine Raven, Emigrant, MT
Zeynep Seyran, Port Jeff. Station, NY
Patricia Smith, Chester, VA

The editors and judges at

New Millennium Writings

are pleased to announce our

NEW MILLENNIUM POETRY AWARD

1ST PLACE
WRITING AWARDS XXXIX

Noah Stetzer

Washington, D.C.

Intruder

1ST PLACE
WRITING AWARDS XL

Claire Bateman

Greenville, SC

Meanwhile, We Called Ourselves Human,

FINALISTS

XXXIX

Devreaux Baker, Mendocino, CA
Patricia B Barone, Fridley, MN
Berwyn Moore Brooker, Erie, PA
Mary Cole, Gloucester, MA
Linda Nemec Foster, Grand Rapids, MI
Anca Hariton, Benicia, CA
Georganne Harmon, Nashville, TN
Linda Lee Harper, Augusta, GA
Alysia Harris, New Haven, CT
Clarinda Harriss, Baltimore, MD
James Heffernan, Hanover, NH
Jo Christiane Ledakis, Miami, FL
Sandy Longley, Delmar, NY
Tim Mayo, Brattleboro, VT
Barbara Mossberg, Eugene, OR
Linwood Rumney, Cincinnati, OH
Anne Stenzel, Richmond, CA
Jim Glenn Thatcher, Yarmouth, ME
Hilde Weisert, Chapel Hill, NC
Ingrid Wendt, Eugene, OR

XL

Carlos A. Bates-Gomez, Forest Hills, NY
Cristina Baptista, Greenwich, CT
Paul Beilstein, Springfield, IL
Lynne Burnett, British Columbia, Canada
Carolyn Evans Campbell, Evergreen, CO
Robert Carr, Orlando, FL
Keith Gaboury, Cambridge, MA
Matthew Hohner, Baltimore, MD
Ellen LaFleche, Northampton, MA
Alison Luterman, Oakland, CA
Djelloul Marbrook, Germantown, NY
Michael Morical, Taipei, Taiwan
Shelley Nelson, Loveland, CO
Emily Newberry, Portland, OR
Elaine Pentalari, Bristol, VT
Sashana Proctor, Cazadero, CA
Robert Sawyer, New York, NY
Jim Glenn Thatcher, Yarmouth, ME
Arminius Tolentino, Portland, OR
Arne Weingart, Chicago, IL

The editors and judges at

New Millennium Writings

are pleased to announce our

NEW MILLENNIUM
FLASH FICTION AWARD

1ST PLACE
WRITING AWARDS XXXIX

Shanna Yetman

Chicago, IL

The Miracle Is to Walk this Earth

1ST PLACE
WRITING AWARDS XL

Alexander Weinstein

Ann Arbor, MI

The Prophet

FINALISTS

XXXIX

Kathleen Arceneaux, Blacksburg, VA
Bailey Brewer, Van Nuys, CA
Isabella David, Ridgefield, CT
Frank duBois, Kalispell, MT
Lili Flanders, Los Angeles, CA
Sherlock Shmees, Cuyahoga Falls, OH
Barbara Fried, Stanford, CA
Paul Kennebeck, Denver, CO
Curt Klinghoffer, Pooler, GA
Frank Pettinelli, Cary, NC
Peter Speziale, New York, NY
Jonathan Segol, Saratoga Springs, NY
Jeanette Quick, Washington, DC
Helia S. Rethmann, Goodlettsville, TN
Maryam Sheikholeslami, Waukesha, WI
John Trout, San Francisco, CA
Bonnie West, Saint Paul, MN
S. E. White, Michigan City, IN
Francine Witte, New York, NY
Melanie Thorne, Petaluma, CA

XL

Brandi Capozzi, Port Murray, NJ
John Corvese, Ontario, Canada
Stan Duncan, Quincy, MA
Paula Friedman, Gresham, OR
Clare Gardner, DPO, AE
Kathleen Hansen, Coronado, CA
Nancy Hanway, Saint Paul, MN
Agatha Hinman, Oakland, CA
Ingrid Jendrzejewski, Vincennes, IN
Deirdra McAfee, Richmond, VA
Jennifer Meng, Taipei City, Taiwan
Kimmo Rosenthal, Schenectady, NY
Giannina Silverman, Bothell, WA
Derry Sampey, Apopka, FL
Vicky Savage, Tampa, FL
Lones Seiber, Morristown, TN
Karen Stromberg, La Mesa, CA
Harold Suretsky, Highland Park, NJ
Rae Theodore, Royersford, PA
Francine Witte, New York, NY

The editors and judges at

New Millennium Writings

are pleased to announce our

NEW MILLENNIUM FICTION AWARD

1ST PLACE
WRITING AWARDS XXXIX

Jackie Davis Martin
San Francisco, CA

Knife

1ST PLACE
WRITING AWARDS XL

Nina Varela
Los Angeles, CA

The Things We Did in Texas

FINALISTS

XXXIX

Leslee Becker, Fort Collins, CO
Thomas Benz, Evanston IL
Thomas Cook, New York, NY
Monte Dutton, Clinton, SC
Jean Garrett, Winslow, ME
Hannah Gildea, Portland, OR
Anna Goodkind, Brooklyn, NY
Jayson Hawkins, Rosharon, TX
Mal King, Santa Paula, CA
Susan Land, Bethesda, MD
Brenda Liebling-Goldberg, Houston, TX
Djelloul Marbrook, Germantown, NY
Wendy Palmer, Oak Bluffs, MA
Terri Scullen, Alexandria, VA
Adam Shafer, Chicago, IL
Margaret Sharma, Alhambra, CA
Lisa Solod, Savannah, GA
Sharon Solwitz, Chicago, IL
Sandi Sonnenfeld, Brooklyn, NY
Matthew Wanner, Coeur D'aLene, ID

XL

Helen Degen Cohen, Deerfield, IL
Joan Corwin, Evanston, IL
John Florio, Brooklyn, NY
Alice Friedman, Fern Park, FL
Adam Golub, Fullerton, CA
Jason Marc Harris, Bryan, TX
Jeannette Hinkle, Melrose, MA
Mark Holden, Chazy, NY
Lorien House, Tijeras, NM
Amanda Kabak, Chicago, IL
Dana Kroos, Las Cruces, NM
Maureen Langloss, NYC, NY
Kathryn Legan, Atlanta, GA
Josh MacIvor-Andersen, Marquette, MI
Sophie Monatte, Hong Kong
Corey Nyhus, Levittown, NY
Shoshana Seidman, Los Angeles, CA
Katherine Sparks, Greenville, VA
Keith Stahl, Syracuse, NY
Julie Weston, Hailey, ID

Poetry • Fiction • Flash Fiction • Nonfiction

NEW MILLENNIUM LITERARY AWARDS

$8,000 in Cash Prizes each Year

+ Publication (online *and* in print)

$1,000 for best Poetry
$1,000 for best Fiction
$1,000 for best Flash Fiction
$1,000 for best Nonfiction

Winners and selected Finalists will be published online *and* in our annual print anthology.

We'd love to read what you've been writing. Submit your best work online at newmillenniumwritings.org, and see our guidelines and mailing instructions on page 267.

hello@newmillenniumwritings.org

CONSECUTIVE WRITING CONTESTS	WRITERS AND POETS PUBLISHED	ANTHOLOGIES DELIVERED	AWARDED TO WRITERS AND POETS
43	1,600+	50,000+	$200,000+

The 25th
Poetry Suite

BOWING TO THE MINISCULE

Tim Mayo

Each day you bow to the family
of fruit flies flitting about
the banana peels of your garbage.
You turn to the mosquito and bless it
with a gentle wave of your hand,
praying it to live without blood.
But it's not enough that you bow to
and bless the miniscule animals
of the world, their oozing larvae.
You must learn to go beyond, to kiss
the cold stone of the mountain, to press
your lips against the invisible beings
of the air, to abide they are there,
yet never swallow their poison,
and you must accept the perennial fly,
its karmic place in your ointment,
the holiness of its presence.

EARLY WARNING SIGNS

Sandy Longley

They mock her at the Quench water cooler;
they call her "Gamma Ray Girl" even though
she's the other side of sixty. She says
she's survived spontaneous combustion.

"Imagine," she whispers, a voice wizened
from lack of use: "compost, steam rising from
a hay stack's surface, acrid tobacco
smell, pistachios bursting from their bins."

I tend to believe her - maybe it's the
scars like pink ribbons rippling above her
breastbone. It can grow cold around the heart;
sometimes we need to self-heat, to embrace
the thermal runaway and then ignite.

When charred torsos are found, she says, there is
usually little sign of struggle.

ELEGY FOR A BAGFUL OF HEARTS

Jo Christiane Ledakis

One hundred-and-two hearts for $2.73
on a black plastic tray,
bought at the meat counter,
on a rainy last Wednesday in November.

Forty-three of them chosen, then chopped,
by a husband, kindly acting as cook,
for the stuffing of the turkey.
More wouldn't fit into the hollowed-out fowl.

Challenged to taste, queasy, mouth dry.
One nipped from the sizzling pan, swallowed,
a single little heart stuck in the throat,
a taste of guillotine in the saliva.

A small bag-o'-hearts,
a mountain of chickens, freshly beheaded,
feet still struggling; they, too, got chopped,
goose-pimpled legs conditioned into finger food.

So much anguish piled in,
convenient, see-through, re-sealable,
until the chosen collectively disappear,
a bunch of mini-Jonases, in the belly of the big bird.

Giving thanks is called for.
Was it not always so:
some hearts, sacrificed
for others' abundant life?

Once, people's hearts were routinely cut out.
Priests sliced into living chests,
pulled out palpitating lumps of flesh,
claimed it was food pleasing the gods;

human sacrifice, thriving
some five hundred years ago,
till someone cleared up the misunderstanding,
promised Heaven much preferred hearts *alive*.

And the left-over fifty-nine?
Can't just throw hearts away!
Cold storage them.
Hearts are used to that.

They clamor for a festive communion,
a redeeming chance
to fittingly honor
a mournful end to short, caged lives.

Unfrozen, the shivery-looking,
bare things were tenderly placed
on a bed of finely cut onion,
sautéed with wild marjoram, sherry,

salt, pepper, expectation, a squirt of cream,
served with toast and garnet Garnacha wine—
yet another occasion to revel
in the good fortune of being alive.

YOU WILL MORPH

Patricia Barone

Whether you're shedding your last egg or the last flaky cell
in your skin's seventh year, or saving all memory of life & poems
upon on a thumb-sized stick, you're in metamorphosis.

Like a caddis fly larva, you've moved
your borrowed snail shell, reed or pebble home upon your back
through air, a medium more permeable than water, impermanent

as decades of childhood, adolescence, the brief day of your majority,
the hours of your adulthood, then the long minutes
of senescence, the moments of your wisdom.

Next is not your death but your metamorphosis:
The itch you've scratched beneath each scapula will be
wing, healing wound, or grace unforeseen—urgent as your heartbeat.

HANDS
(from Morocco)
Georganne Harmon

Here, beyond the sea that halves us
I sink my hands deep into couscous
three times, reaching across waves
to you. With time, with silence,
the grain swallows water three times
and three times increases
and becomes whole.

I miss the skin
you lay against my skin,
your hand's expanse
on my open back,
the warm envelope of you.

My hands touch and turn
the barley, semolina,

then the corn—three rounds—
then choose carrots, zucchini, turnips.
They will be succulent in my mouth,
handed in, cradled as if
we were tasting it together,
all skins blending, nourishing
like a story's bones linked
and told in the dark.

I FORGOT MY POEM TODAY

Mary Davies Cole

went right out of my head
but i could hear it rustling
in the leaf-strewn scratch of lawn
between my house and the white one
next door where the woman way older
than i am is planning her next
marathon uphill with one hand
tied behind her back

(and she never loses anything)

i am clapping my hands
to bring back the dog who,
like the poem, was also forgotten
and has taken off

       elusive beasts –
       the two of them

       come here now poem!
       this never works

you end up writing about nothing
while silence dances all about you
and your poem is halfway to Kansas

(perhaps it will stop in Iowa City
to improve itself)

i listen intently for its return,
waiting to hear its feet composing themselves
out in the garage while the dog,
who is now home, bangs its tail in time
against the garbage can.

i am waiting for the poem to sing its song
so i can catch the meter
snag the line and
hear the music of it all but

my poem *howls*
out there in the wilderness

and this is my fault
for losing it in the first place

poems do not come home
when you rattle the dog biscuit jar
this may be why many people,
(perhaps most)
prefer dogs
to poems.

ON THE BLUED CANVAS AND THEN IN A CAVE

Linda Lee Harper

the sailboat hovers between
the virgin forest banked around
the purple mountain barely
sketched in enough to see shape
and the water waiting for grays
the way a good gravy needs
thickening before it looks right.

Already scratched into that
grounded cloth, it's easy to see
clouds muscling in
where haze hangs so high
it's not clear if it's cloth
breaking through the blue
slightly browned to dull its gleams

sent straight from some
divinity of beginning painters,
OR it's an inadvertent drip from
a new filbert cheaper than
the next one will be, this effort,
this landscape copied from
a card, the one she never sent

a friend who seemed like the
sky beyond the titanium white
of both boat and snowy ridge,
to fade ever more into distance,
a friend whose smile seemed to
flatten and merge with a horizon line
eyes pained to follow like brush

strokes trailing off the edge of the world.

But if it's in a cave that you think best,
then by all means, hunker down,
burrow in and seek the damp
where the wisest of bats hang
their hats, even if upside down.

I want you to excel at philosophy,
I want you to succeed at math.
I want all the answers to come
to you with minimal effort.
If in that primal darkness, quiescent,

where fish with blind eyes swim,
you find the best interiors you
possess, then by all means,
fill your mouth with dark space
that underground shares willingly.

If what crawls over stone feels
at home, where sleek tails slide
across your open hands like
braided whips, remain and send
memos to those upside,

to those who remember your
smile as slick as a moon peeling
itself into the night's open palm,
the one you fail to offer up to light,
poor pilgrim lost to time and creed.

THE UPRIGHT PIANO

After *Piano on Fire* by Andrew Ferez

Hedy Habra

I see myself out in the cold, draped in a silk nightgown,
seated barefoot on a stool by that upright piano, you
know, the one my mother bought when she thought I
should take piano lessons, while others played during
recess, oh, how I first struggled striking notes daily,
practicing scales, then rehearsing Mozart's "Rondo
alla Turca" till I'd play it in my mind relentlessly, *tan
tan tan . . . tan tan tan . . .* even when I knew I'd never
learn another piece, and now, half a century later, I am
drawing with memory's wavering lines that same piano
to make it the vessel of my heart's message, of so much
left unsaid buried in a bitter well turning into notes that
rise in tongues of cold fire licking my insides with every
key I touch, unharmed, I feel the piano ablaze under
my fingertips, twisted candles adorn its top that grows
into a tower and turrets spouting flames from windows,
a menace to the adjacent branches, my fingers wildly
strike the keyboard while the sky opens up like a stage
filled with shimmering damask memories dancing to the
melody like maddened fireflies.

First published by *Knot Magazine*
From *Under Brushstrokes* (Press 53, 2015)

IN LIEU OF A CHRISTMAS LETTER,

Ingrid Wendt

this excuse for a poem, which may never be sent. Nearly forty
years we've been on time, have mined each past year's calendar for news,
good cheer, and now we draw a blank. Here, we're living from storm
to storm in the small retreat we've owned for 30 years and soon

will try to sell, or not. We talk. Everything we've ever known
is upside down. My balance isn't good, I fall. The same wars
go on, each day reports come in of deaths our country will not own,
and Ruth's, the slowest train in all creation chugging towards

her for months? Hope? Something burned and crusted on the stove,
at war with guilt when I succumb to sudden moments of renewal
as when – after the enormous storm that took away homes, roads,
took trees it its jaws and dropped them onto our own neighbors' roof—

I went walking late one night on the beach, went wading right through
knee-high, washed up sea-foam quivering, shimmering: millions
of the tiniest possible bubbles, like jellyfish, spangling my boots
(boots bought for me by a man so faithful a companion

planets in their orbits could be jealous), my boots from arches
all the way to knees were—ah, the wonder—bandaged in stars.

This poem was originally published online in the
journal, *Cascadia Review*, Spring, 2014.

UNDER THE SIGN OF KRONOS
—(March 6, 1988)

Jim Glenn Thatcher

Tonight I stood outside and watched two planets
In a near-conjunction that will not occur again
For another thousand years: The bright slow glide
Of Venus and Jupiter; brilliant, steady;
Drawn together in a long-determined arc
Down the west and into the endless night
That always sleeps the circling world.

While over all Orion towered
Shining in the south, master of this night
Whose stars and galaxies knew more of time
Than any planet ever will. Watchful hunter,
Bow drawn back, aimed into the darkness
Of an eternity far beyond our own,
The time coming when his stars will have dispersed
Into another form—or forms—or formlessness—
Long after the passing of my kind,
Lovers of the same earth, the same light,
The same dream gone long into its night
When Orion hunts no more.

Later, behind closed lids, locked in the trance
Of meditation, I silently awaited
The conjuration of whatever was to come in the stars
Born visible from the vastnesses of my skull
And suddenly remembered the myth of Kronos,
Father of the gods, who rose from darkness
And devoured his children as they were born.

And then I saw great waves of flame billowing
As though from bright hot solar storms, sweeping out
To fall curling back upon themselves; great crescents
Licking endlessly at their own underbellies—
Great tear-drop orbs of fire—each ebbing
Its own shadow back into itself—its own demise,
Its own night, its own extinction. Toward that night
When Forever has burned itself away, and time
Has gone full circle, back to the sign of Kronos.

SPECKS IN THE OINTMENT

Jim Glenn Thatcher

In the pre-dawn gloom of my waking
A fly is attempting to speak to me.
An early fly, a most unseasonable fly.
A pink, distinctly human tongue struggles
against the mangling bites of furious mandibles.
It is trying to tell me something of our common nature,
a relationship which I do not want and did not ask for.
Its buzzing irritates me almost beyond endurance,
yet the false compassion of courtesy bids me
to listen for speech I suspect but cannot hear.

In the thousand reflections of each eye
I recognize the sufferings of a fellow being.
In each facet quivers a different image—
a spider, the ceiling, my own distorted features,
the lamp, the dresser, all the kaleidoscopic
commonplaces of our mutual situation.

I strain my own eyes toward him, seeking larger meanings.
I want to experience the profundity of this moment.
I want irrefutable evidence of spiritual connection,
a distinct sign in each refraction of his vision:
a planet warm and turning, for instance,
or a tiny moon in orbit, frowning, and beyond the moon
galaxies whirling pinwheels of delight.
But I see only the ranks of my own mirrored features
staring back in their agonized legions.

So much I could tell him. So much hope to be given:
In these latitudes the manure of south-facing pastures is far richer
than the sun-deprived patties of the northern slopes.
A dead fox lies in the alders behind our neighbor's barn.
It is March. The mud time is coming.
New seed will soon take, and our fortunes lie fallow.
Under the frozen sod lie regions of great turmoil and transformation.

CHASMOPHILE

Berwyn Moore

I crawled from the wet meat
of the womb to the dark fuzz

of a blanket over my head
to cardboard slitted with holes,

the flashy wheels it contained
lost in tinsel and ripped paper.

An army of coats in the attic
held me captive in musky fur

and naphthalene, a canopy of lilacs
drowsed me, and the high crook

of a mulberry branch muffled
the whirr of my mother's voice.

Family gossip dropped like crumbs
from the table, where underneath

I hunkered amid the stockinged
and lion-pawed legs. In the barn,

I crept through hay tunnels,
seed pods still green and pungent,

the dark so complete I struck
a match, saw no mouse or snake

to filch the air, then sizzled
the flame in spit. How lovely

the absence of light and voice
in a square of space no bigger

than a pout. My breath slowed.
My bones melted as I curled

up—a delinquent smudge—
blind and blissful in not knowing.

WHAT DOES IT TAKE

Doris Ivie

What does it take to be ready to die?
Legal dispersal of shirts and shekels?
Reviewing lost moments in bright surround-sound?
Telling someone you love her, no matter what?
Making amends for every sin you can remember,
as well as those you don't?
Or is it loving your crackly old self,
realizing breath can break away
and all your light is slipping up that silver cord
until what was you lies there, electrons untamed.

HIC SUNT DRACONES

Annie Stenzel

My offer to sleep without blankets
until you are warm
strikes you as odd. *Will you starve
when I'm hungry? Lie awake if I'm
restless?* you ask me. I scowl and nod.

That was the part of the dream
I held on to, and groped for my pen
to record in the dark. *My love
is not even: it's awkward*, I write
with a wavering hand. Someone sobs.

Rough times in this dream life:
the waters are wicked, the symbols
unclear. I play several roles.
Once I throttled myself
while I watched with great horror;

tried to cry *wait—I'm dangerous*
but no one could hear. Years ago
with a fever I strayed into rough country—
no map, no guide, but I got out
alive. Trouble is, now the place looks like

home when I wake up—and you?
I have no idea who you are.

TO CHRISTOFORO COLUMBUS
—before dawn*[1]

Anca Hariton

Christoforo, can you hear me if I whisper?
It is late and clad bones need sleep.
I know you're watching though—
even if they think you're dream ruled—.
Can you see me?
Si, si, la Donna ti visita.*[2]
I commune with the seas now conquered, unconquered,
                         conquered, unconquered
      …wasn't that what the waves called to you?

Some grow their crest high
land and never leave. Yet roiling waters do
christen when voyaged, imprint with another power
gust giving, restless, fraternal.
You heard them prattle and pray
over fish bones, wish bones,
                  fish bones, wish bones
      …isn't that what whitens us?

No wonder that pilgrims seek to root their faith
if they hold, a forest protects their halo, carries the cargo
across and if you knew the path of this pregnancy,
Christoforo, you may have not left
new world expectant, delivery, delivered
                delivery, delivered
      …wasn't that how the sea curled around you?

When the shots aimed farther,
and treading, you asked where
Where are you, God?
stared at the compass dance,
West? then lost again, *Where are you...where*
                where are you...are you
     ...wasn't that what the tide was also searching?

Remember, Christoforo, I have but this candle
to carry us through the night.
Can you see flame forward
years bilge from shipping flesh, gun, gold, history rising
following smoke masts, enslaving, unslaving,
               enslaving, unslaving,
     ...wasn't that what the foams foretold?

They called *freedom*, but she was not ready to adorn,
shores, not your nor mine—blood cannot be washed—
only birth righted, heart brushed
by deeper loss or gain, five hundred spokes or more
in years wheeling, decoding, encoding,
             decoding, encoding
     ...did you see their scroll exacting the mist?

And what is left, right?
Peace, Christoforo, off-springs shall peruse these sands
cover your ears, fill in your footsteps—wine of pardon—
while pride on nightmares mounted
be loosened away, scatter and salt,
            scatter and salt
     ...for waves to heave, deepen their sigh.

So rest now by the dawn's oar
mio caro figlio*3) ,
I just needed to touch you,
christen you afresh
in ardour married calm, a rdour...marri ed...ca lm...
a...ma(e)ri...ca...

....

Author's Notes:

[1] Christoforo Columbus had been bedridden with high fever for days, on the way back to Spain from his first voyage to the New World. During a stormy night, the young aid providing him with daily food and fresh water heard fragments of conversation and moans from the Captain's cabin. Soon after, rumors spread on the ship about this having been a visitation from his mother, who—that very night—gave her son, Christoforo, the strength to survive.

[2] **(Italian)** *The lady visits you.*

[3] **(Italian)** *My dear son*

....

TRAINWRECK, MINNEAPOLIS (A LOVE POEM)

Arne Weingart

I felt the sound before I heard it,
a cone of noise with vast ambition
but nothing in back of it but silence,
the kind that comes after calamity.

The train stopped short after
having dragged the car catty-corner
into the crossing. The point of impact
was the front passenger door and

window, shards of which were
being pulled delicately out of the
arm and shoulder of the woman
who sat on the curb, blood, but

not too much blood, leaking into
a handkerchief wrapped around
her wrist. The boy still sat quietly
in the backseat, thinking about

the continuous collisions he rehearsed
with toy train and toy train,
toy car and toy truck, toy car and
toy train until the man came and

plucked him up into the world again,
where, in the distance, you could hear
sirens, many sirens approach
and converge. Does it matter that

this was the same train on the same track
that I was planning to take later
to the airport? No, it does not.
And what was the man thinking

who drove his family across the tracks?
What thought could possibly be big enough
to lose track of a train in? Driving along,
I've had that same thought myself.

Lucky, I guess, to know a woman
who won't think twice about
yelling at me, you fool, before I go and
drive us off the edge of the earth.

THE ICE STORM

Linwood Rumney

It isn't tenderness that sometimes
compels water to press itself so firmly
against the landscape, like the too-cold hand
set upon a lover's belly to startle

and amuse. Trees break from the weight
of this embrace. As in spring, through
a trick of light, low-hanging branches
seem to fracture as they dip below

the river's surface. But there's no error
of appearance here. This season is literal.
Something lost all patience with shadows
and casts them out with clarity

that stuns for its accumulated
barrenness. Mornings, children skate
in driveways, parents gather ice to flush
toilets while the radio catalogs, as though

at war, the losses of the day before:
one trailer collapsed, killing the sole
inhabitant; another bridge declared
impassable; and half the state cut off

from the power grid. Residents
are advised to boil water, to ventilate
running generators, to stay away
from windows and off the roads. Later,

there will be interviews with the woman
who gave birth in a car flipped over
in a ditch, the octogenarian
who burned furniture for heat in his

living room, and the fortunate couple who,
visiting friends when the storm began,
were not at home when an ice swell
dragged the whole thing into the river.

THIS THING WE CALL FRIENDSHIP IS BIGGER THAN WE KNOW

Barbara Mossberg

Luna the whale aka L98 or Tsuux'iit, wanted only to
be our friend. Every day, the Canadian Department
of Fisheries and Oceans said, she got into trouble:
the more she tried to engage us, the more she was an
outlaw. Humans—Mowachaht/Muchalaht First Nation,
journalists, teachers, tourists—were written up. Cited.
Booked. Their crime—and they did get fined: it was
looking the whale in the eye. Looking was proscribed.
By law, no one could relate to the whale. Ignore it—the
official policy. And yet the whale did not understand. It
swam up to the boats, grabbed a hose with its mouth,
and sprayed the folks on deck. It made all its entreating
sounds. Don't look at it, people were told. Look away.
You are robbing it of its whale-ness. It never can become
a real whale and go back to a pod life if you allow it to
experience humans as its community. But some came
to believe that ignoring the whale was cruel. They felt
criminally implicated. One man finally decided—he
was a writer—Luna (it was a he) wants friendship. It
was like Huckleberry Finn: *I'll go to hell! I will look him
in the eye. Come what may.* I'm not going to say here
that the government backed off, in the face of citizen
insurrection, civic insurgency, and that it was a happy
ending. Well, it was a happy ending, but it is not one
that saved the whale's life. They wanted to imprison the
whale, cage it as a danger. The First Nation, eldercare, the
elementary school, used song and dance to encourage
the whale to resist capture. It was a tug of war, engines vs.
boats paddled by grade-school singers, secretaries,

wrinkled matriarchs, it was government vs. the people. It was we the people as at first, at last. A whale who wanted to be a friend broke down the boundaries of who we are as people, extending enfranchisement to species with a big heart. A journalist who came for three weeks to report on the goings on stayed three years, called to friendship. He said, "This thing we call friendship is bigger than we know." Certainly Luna was the biggest friend he had. It turns out we learn about friendship from a slippery and leaping creature, and that the possibilities for friendship are infinite in this universe. Luna was killed by a tugboat's propeller—the fishermen they said hated the whale and wanted it dead—but here we see, none of us who watched the news reports wanted this whale dead. We all felt we were its friend. We all cried to lose him. Our lives were changed. He was the friendship teacher. Oh, yes, this is the happy ending. We learned about friendship, something bigger than we know.

GOD WHO WATCHES THE SPARROWS
Laura Still

A tall man, a woman who watches her step,
we walk up hill from the Garonne
—just in time I notice
patch of gray-brown, not moss or stone
but feathers. I bend; meet a reptilean eye:
Bonjour, mon bebe—qu'est-ce tu fait?

Ee-eep!
which if you don't speak bird,
translates: *fallen from my nest,
can't get up.* My love inspects,
takes out his camera.
I scan overhanging branches,
top of wall, for a distressed (even
aggressive) mother hovering—nothing.

What can we do? Not walk away, with
100 cats in the neighborhood. *Don't!*
as he stretches his hand to it—
once as a child I picked up a fallen bird
only to feel its heart stop. He flattens
his fingers on rough cobbles, coaxes
the nestling to perch on them.

Same moment:
I spy a twig-stuffed hole above, almost
beyond reach. My long-limbed *amour* boosts
himself on a crevice, extends his slight burden
upward, tiny wings flutter,
lift, minute talons grasp wisps
of dangling wood,
scramble home.

FOX TRACKS
Clarinda Harriss

This morning fox tracks crosshatched my porch
right up to kitchen. Maybe the fox hoped
my father would feed him a chicken bone.
Some folks in backwoods Carolina long ago
called foxes half cat and half dog
for the way they slink low to the ground,
their pretty faces giving nothing away.
Some even called foxes kin to ghosts
for how you can watch and watch them
and they disappear right before your eyes.
Today in my city back yard the fox was all dog,
dozing in the sun, rousing only to nip a flea,
lick his balls, snuggle deeper into his great tail.
My father called the fox he half-tamed Gutch
for how he was tough and brave and no way
human, fearless during mating season, ki-i-i-i
his only word.
             So I could send what I saw
to my father in a dream I pressed a picture
of the fox onto the back of my eyeballs, and
tonight my father lured Gutch into my sleep.
I asked my father if it was true that Gutch
fed from his hand.   My father answered,
It's true that I told you so. Then k-i-i-i-I,
a blink and both of them had gone to earth.

LADY

Alison Luterman

Not the term we fought for, which was *woman*—
a word with woe and a man in it, low

and close to the ground—lifter of pots, hauler of feed
to the barn. But *Lady,* from Middle English: *loaf,*

or *dough*; woman as yeasty, life-giving substance, also,
let's face it, monied: mistress of the house, Lady

Abbondanza, the Bountiful one, aswim in flowing hair.
Lady Godiva rode through town, famously bare

and unashamed. Lady Murasaki invented the novel
to amuse her sister ladies-in-waiting at the Imperial Court;

they passed pages to each other like forbidden love notes.
I knew a woman whose mad mother would run

to Mount Tamalpais, the Sleeping Lady,
whenever she escaped the mental ward.

She died there, sheltered in its shadow,
curled in on herself like a fiddle-head fern.

I like to see our young girls
dress like ladies, school principal, Dr. Goodrich

said in 1969, when he sent Valerie Franks home
for wearing a blue velvet pantsuit in sixth grade.

She was ahead of her time. In college I read *Portrait of a Lady*
and threw the book against the wall in rage,

because the heroine was so soft and creamy,
a frilled pastry in the marriage-market,

trying to get eaten before she grew stale.
My own mother could be overheard on the phone

with an unwise telemarketer: "And *don't* call me honey!" Slam.
She kept her curly hair cropped short, like a Roman boy,

wore no make-up, and did not aspire
to the despised, coveted term, so I didn't either,

though Lady Day wore a white gardenia tucked behind her ear
and the bruised gin of her voice enticed the stars.

Years later, when I moved to the city, those ladies of the night
entranced me, leaning into open cars on International,

teetering on platform heels. Mornings I'd find spent condoms
in the parking lot, but the ladies themselves were shut up tight

like reverse morning glories, stripped
of maquillage and wigs: no glitter,

no shoulder, no moon.
I wanted to follow the youngest one up to her room

and watch over her while she slept, I was a kept
woman at the time, lady of the house, wanna-be poet,

taking all day to buy melons at the farmer's market.
Then, divorce: I was a working girl again, striding through the Mission

in my seven-league boots, stepping over piles of dogshit
and huddled bodies to get to the train, Stunned to find myself alive,

strong, and lonely. Later still I was the visiting poet;
kids called me "the poetry lady", and sometimes

"Mrs. Poem"—lugging a two-ton satchel full of lesson plans
over an aching shoulder. How many lives

do we live in one body? I wanted a child
of my own. None came, and life went on,

years of it: a new marriage, a few cats.
Kwan Yin, the Compassionate Lady,

hears the cries of the world and responds.
Deep in middle age, I found myself

in a ritual circle of dancing women when the leader asked us
to take the position of one giving birth. It seemed

impossible. And yet, when I tried,
the Lady appeared before me at last,

as a squat, black, obsidian statue, well past first youth
but garlanded with fresh flowers.

Is there a message? the leader asked. I am not the type
to expect an answer, but

Love your babies, I heard the Lady say, as clear
as sunlight or birdsong. What babies? I asked.

So she said it again. All my mind's progeny
appeared to me then: written

and unwritten. I thought also of those whom I loved,
and those whom I had failed,

as well as my never-born
children and incompletely-grieved-for dead.

I started to weep, then wail, sobs
passing through me like lives

I might have lived. *Everyone
is my baby!* I cried. *Yes*, the Lady said.

She didn't look like a lady.
She seemed earth itself, open and rough.

Uncompromising. *Love your babies*,
she kept insisting, until I was done for.

THE FISHERMAN'S WIFE

C. Ann Kodra

Ask for too much,
and you'll end up nattering away
at what you meant to love. Bigger, better,

we all believe we need it to reel in bliss.
She longed for a cottage, a castle, a kingdom.
Floundering, her husband groveled for more until

she believed only in the power of fishing line
strong enough to pull up the sun,
a sinker to drown the moon.

As he brought home wish after wish roiling with gray
wrath, what she meant to say—red kerchief
bobbing with the weight of each desire—was

Bring me your heart swelled with saltwater
from an ocean neither you nor I
could ever drain.

FIELD OF BULLETS, MEDICINE BOW

Armin Tolentino

> The Field of Bullets hypothesis describes a model in
> which extinction is non-selective and occurs randomly.
> The metaphor suggests that species are simply out in a
> field and "bullets" are hitting them at random, thus their
> extinction operates without relation to their adaptability.

Forty five dollars of regular unleaded.
My gas tank is a graveyard on fire.
Most every species that once drew breath
is fossil now, or oil. If I'm to die
in this latest Apocalypse, what would my body
ignite? Whose escape could I fuel?

Wyoming, too, is an unmarked grave
and the wind shears off an inch
each year to flash the bones of another
failure felled by the hard hand of cataclysm.
All my escape routes are paved
on the backs of a billion extinctions.

As the Cretaceous closed,
did You gather Your children
in a field to graze while You scooped
in Your two open palms, the width
of continents, a handful of celestial stones
to scatter like snowflakes upon their gaping
mouths?

Or did You close one eye
and aim?

MIRACLE

Lynne Burnett

Is it a miracle
that I found the worm in time—
having gone into my den much earlier
than usual, to turn the computer on—
and saw the dark, exhausted thread of its
body lying in the middle of a desert
of beige carpet, picked it up, barely moist, and
laid it outside on the wet grass, and watched
until it finally waved goodbye at one end,
easing itself into the darkness it knows?

Or is the miracle
that the annelid slid
through sealed doors and windows
to get inside my house in the first place,
that it became a finger pointing
from the Buddha's hand,
laying at my feet its five paired hearts
and the power of intervention—
of life continued
or of death without comment?

Is there a day without its miracle,
for doesn't one follow the other
because of a vast accordion of worms
playing now the soil's anthem, now its dirge,
burrowing through millennial darknesses
so plants can breathe and grow, and
become the planet's green lungs feeding
the body of this world, each inhabitant
still part of that first inspiration:
the good air of life lived, wholly inspired.

"Miracle" was first published in the Aug/Sept
'06 issue of *North Shore Magazine*.

RIVER SWIMMING

Shelley Kitchura Nelson

Her voice is a rough river crashing into rocks,
                    bumping the shoreline,
                stopping then starting again;
            catching her breath,
        continuing on into tributaries
and creeks that lead to the delta.
        The river is a story with paragraphs
                leading to other paragraphs
                    and chapters that for minutes
                        have nothing to do with where they began.
                Her voice quivers and skips a beat in every sentence.
            Brimming with despair, her story rolls on;
        don't leave me,
    don't hang up,
        don't wander from my words.
                The news that has nothing to do with the time we have to talk;
                    streaming updates on her friends' illnesses,
                        her appointments and to do lists –
                    her dog's daily and nightly rituals.
            Nothing is really new.
        So the river flows on and I listen
    for the flood.

The river's edge rises with much needed rain.
                    Muddy rushing water, trees, boulders, homes, debris,
                memories release from her mouth,
            losing articulation along the way
        after years of stability,
knowing what will be destroyed.
        Paths agreed to that she must share, even with all the mess it creates.
            People leave, friends disappear, families hide.
                Weeks go by without a call to see if the river has receded yet.
                    Life becomes unstable and her voice more anxious.
            I use to need her voice.
        The river that flowed from her mouth was smooth,
            effortless with life. Refreshing.
It helped me see the ocean through its tributaries, creeks and deltas.
        I swam in that river and she held me in her arms and rocked me with gentle waves.
            I heard the lovely sound that takes over when swimming beneath the surface;
                that rush of water filling your ears – some think loud, I think not.
                I will love the river even in the midst of this flood.
            Aware that the plight will worsen,
        I will find a strong fallen branch,
    hold on until it tears away and
I can swim free.

BORN LOVERS OUT OF WATER

Sashana Kane Proctor

They are all born lovers out of water. In the very moment she steps over the edge of her bathtub, clambering out of still warm water, everyone the woman knows is emerging from the wet born into love.

The woman's friend braces her hands on the edge
of the swimming pool and pushes herself out of
the water dripping cares pulling honeyed air into
hungry lungs long muscles well used ravenous
for fan of summer salad her husband splays
for her at home already dreaming her scrappy
orange cat onto her evening lap. In the depths
of her darkness the woman's sister raises her face
from the washbowl dripping tears and water
her reflection rivulet in the looking glass. She
sustained only by pinpoint of being folded away
so deep she can't feel it. The walls of the woman's
neighbor run wet with unshed tears as he lets the
TV judge watch him. His collecting pool floats
the body of his long dead difficult wife reflects his
son out of work and out of his understanding his
daughter shoved by melancholia off the high dive
of success. He wonders where is the life vest so no
one drowns. On a far bank where crystal waters
race the mother bear has slapped her cub into the
fracas of bears and froth and flashing fish and now
savors soft flesh click of bone rush of flavor between
her teeth. The woman's daughter shoves from the
nearby creek bottom and rushes surface tension
and gulps the sky loving cool of skin and stroke
of sun chestnut hair streaming a second snatched
from hustle. From a tank cupping 10,000 gallons of
cool translucent water the woman's beloved slides
his hands from wet blessing he knows so well. He
is seeing the water he stewards pushed up the

mountain to storage tanks at the top and watching it flow through pipes and out of faucets and into glasses and down throats and he is saying thank you. Meanwhile the woman's cousin is shoving through soggy thick of a radiator Missouri morning. She is being walked by the tail thumping sassy quizzical self possessed tongue lolling black and white dog wonder of her life. The one who taught her when people couldn't that love is a constant cord. The woman's granddog drops his log into the creek on purpose to dive his muzzle deep through water mirror and emerge with a foot of drippy wood on either side of his mouth. The dog is looking for his man to watch him but he is not there. His man the woman's son is a masked and sweating sentinel near his love as a surgeon reaches into gushing pond of womb to take up their slippery fish of boychild in whose eyes the man sees that he is newborn. The woman's aunt who was ninety-three floats from her body that was almost all water and then sighs into a slipstream of wellness shrugging it on like a sweater in the cool. She chuckles a burble of love onto the heads of her grown children the beads of her being and then is gone.

And the woman steps from her bath. In the well of herself the lover born of this.

AN EPITHALAMIUM

Robert A.B. Sawyer

What is marriage but a counting down
from the infinite to the ultimate?

1.

The lover and beloved aligned, two parallel lives
Meet at a place known only to themselves.
They are agreed:
There are no heroes except lovers, no great act except love.
If there is a door one will knock and one will answer.
So long as their eyes are open, no crowd can conceal the one from the other.

2.

I am struck by the lovers' modesty.
How they require our presence here to test the adhesive
They've mixed in the dark and applied with their own moisture.
Love is so much greater than the sum of its nouns,
Superlatives and verbs.
But the wait to show it can seem interminable.
Now, here, among the witnesses, the wait is over.

It is here at last; present in the smallest
Nearly imperceptible gesture.
All caught by the ever alert lovers—
The light in the eye, a lure,
The mouth, a net.

3.

To look so closely is to see, to listen so intensely is to hear,
To note is to praise.
The gods of love are capricious at best, on occasion, sadistic,
But they deserve our praise.

In love, we are like a man or a woman who once hungry as a child
Remains hungry all his or her life.
Now, as husband and wife, feed your lover
Feed your beloved
Lick your plates clean.

BUDDHIST SCHOOL OF COSMETOLOGY: LESSON ONE

Elaine Pentaleri

Without fatigue a candle burns
and sings inaudibly,
illuminates a small place
against an immeasurable counterpart of unlit space.
A cat in all its soft fur nudges my neck,
unembarrassed at its blatant showing of need.
I pet and purr in small places;
This small world I inhabit.
Meanwhile, the stars drone like bees.

At times the trees
that continually redecorate the landscape
are neither beautiful nor ugly.
As I look at them, they disappear.
At times the whorl of space defies mathematics.
The maps of geometry scratch
at immeasurable dimension.

At birth I broke
into a smaller paradigm,
defined a world through senses,
clutched the air,
grew accustomed to the load roar
of my own breathing.

The small places of candles shed light upon something;
They butt up against the dark.
Without emotion I empty
myself to the questions.

Yesterday. There was music from a piano,
flooding space, moving like water.
A thing of this world,
And such a soft perfection of limber hands,
A beauty such as I could hardly bear,

I am turned inside out.

Yesterday was   now   it isn't anymore.
The dishes are dirty. I made them that way. I wash them.
After opening the bottle of wine, we drank it.
Soon, it was empty.
All continually becomes undone.

After the music, the hands, after the undoing, what.
Something I choose to name Beauty, or Power,
Something extending beyond this circle of light,
Beyond geometry
is/or.
From where this pull, this turning inside out,
and what for and why.
I do not want to sleep   again.
The night grows larger. The dishes are clean.
Tomorrow will come as it always does,
There will be breakfast, and other things to be undone.
On the way to work the mountains and the trees
will spread right there in front of my eyes, beautifully.
I will not hear the drone of stars.

SAUDADE: 1983

Matt Hohner

for Phil, Brian, and Steve

February

The weathermen had tracked its march across
the continent for days, watched it scoop moisture
from the gulf and turn up the coast, slamming
into winter so hard it exploded snow. They said
it wasn't a blizzard, but we knew different.
Thundersnow and sleet and lightning swirling
above our soaked and frigid fingers, we shaped
the nor'easter into a room four boys could cram their
hearts into. We were powerful, solid in all that white,
self-reliant in snow pants and extra socks and eyes
tearing in the icy wind. Down in that little gully
by the kitchen of Steve's father's church, we made our
stand against God and nature's anger, working stinging
hands that were well past frozen, our toes long given
away to frost inside our ice-block boots. Panting steam
like thoroughbreds, we crawled inside our polar womb.
Cross-legged in silence against the history raging
around us, we saw the work in each other's faces,
the four of us feeling for the first time the real
potential packed in our arms. We sat a long time
in that hut, knowing the use of work, listening to the
violence of what waited for us outside, emerging
just as the winds died to struggle our separate ways
home through waist-high drifts to warm living rooms
and baths, and steaming mugs of instant chocolate.
That night we plummeted into achy sleep, never more
alive, having met peril bigger than us and made it ours.

June

In June we were all sweat and shovels,
delving ourselves down into the cool ground,
covered up by plywood and old rugs and earth
in the back corner of Steve's yard between forsythia
and white pine, where the neighbor's fence dissolved
in barbs and rust. We sat in the darkness, talked of
girls and bikes and music. We wore brown clods home
to dinner in our hair and under our nails, a bucketful
in each shoe, ochre clay smeared into our shirts.
I think often of our fort with its rooms and alcoves,
shelves carved into side walls, candle chimneys
and food stashes, nestled between roots. Alive
in that subterranean shadow world, we dug our
collective grave together, escaping life above
for a little while, for just long enough.

August

That last August Saturday morning before
we returned to gym uniforms and lunch money
and homework for another school year, Steve's
brother Howard drove us in the squeaky yellow
Chevy Nova with black pleather seats that melted
onto the backs of our bare thighs and dropped us
off upstream, ten miles north into horse country.
Shoulders slung with fat old truck tire tubes, we
descended the weedy banks to the Gunpowder,
low in spots after weeks of drought, and set
ourselves into the clear currents. Summer

leaned over us from the riverbanks, green-dappled
and leafy, silent and still. In the cooler, humid
stream bottom, Converse All-Stars reeking
of algae and swelter and soaked through, our
heels trailed vees behind us as we drifted
backwards towards autumn, aimless as leaves.

Rambling awkward as foals over pebbled shallows
and ages, chuting fast down the old wooden mill
race between boulders, we were still boy enough
for splash battles and laughter, skipping flat
stones, and mooning everything that moved.

Each of us was Huckleberry Finn. Each of us
was runaway Jim. High school and college and real
work loomed like cops and grandfathers, but we
held the years before us at arms' length, shut our
eyes, floated across those waning hours like
milkweed silk. Covered in dreams and lies, we
leaned our ears into the distance for a sound
that would call us away to ourselves from
futures that would choose us, from the
demons we would not outgrow.

HOW I LOST YOUR POEMS

Michael Morical

Your book arrived in extra padding
the morning I went to Jones Beach.
I stuffed it in my daypack
to read your sonnets by the sea,
to ride the meter riding me.

But first I swam, having stashed your work
in my waterproof pack where a box of blueberries
spilled a summer or two ago,
blotching my New Yorker cover, torn
from the rest, of course, by rummaging.

And while I breast-stroked back to shore,
a seagull pecked your poems, tearing
lines, ripping images, swallowing words.
What would I tell you?
How had a birdbrain unzipped the zipper?

When the thief sensed my urgency,
it grabbed a wad of verse
in its beak and flew out with the undertow.
Who knows where it landed, or if?
Can you send another copy?

MEDITATION FOR EGGS

Ellen LaFleche

Begin with the fimbria – those long elegant fallopian fingers.
Dream them luring the egg, luring it with their slow
hypnotic beckoning: *come to me, come to me.*
How the egg, mesmerized, tumbles into the tube.

Dream a couple standing in their bedroom.
How the woman's lover holds her aloft.
Dream her mating in the air like a hummingbird,
all trembling colors and weightless coming.
Nectar-lipped, she dips and dips,
her pelvis shivering in the overhead mirror like a pair of wings.

A woman, abandoned at sixty.
Dream her carrying a basket of wash down shivering cellar steps.
How tears sluice through her wrinkles like gutter water,
how they pool in the smile lines that bracket her mouth.
Dream her remembering when smile lines bracketed her other,
more joyous mouth.
Dream her uterus, that old egg basket, savoring the memory of yolk and blood.

Re-dream the hummingbird woman.
How she walks near the Seine,
her scarf's metallic threads sparking silver, sparking blue.
Sparking green, aqua, aquamarine.
Dream the evening sun descending into the Seine,
its reflection splitting in half like a fertilized ovum.

Re-dream the woman abandoned at sixty.
How she remembers sweat and nectar on her lover's mouth.
Dream the scarf that protects the ruby scar on her throat,
its silver threads glinting under the diner's fluorescent light.
Dream her carrying eggs and hash browns to a long-distance trucker.

Dream the female hummingbird hovering over her nest.
How her lustrous wings hum,
how they hum, hum,
a steady melody for the eggs in her cup-shaped nest.

FERGUSON

Emily Pittman Newberry

The street is bored red even
if the cameras are shocked
to see another misdemeanor
drying in the afternoon sun.

An hour ago skate boards
scratched out hip hop songs
on sidewalk staves with short
notes and no rests, only repeats.

The day didn't mean to make
trouble, but it couldn't help
asking if what came yesterday
might please, politely disappear.

Still, it will make for riveting
reality TV when the anger
of the stopped and searched
finds a good place

to strike. One match and the
cold steel of the lawfully blind
rules will burn around
police vans and convenience

stores. The cameras roll.
"Take one," the rioters say.
And the body lies out behind
yellow tape, dreaming.

WALRUS

Robert S. Carr

Dedicated to the protesters who suspended
themselves from the St. Johns Bridge
to block the passage of Shell Oil's icebreaker
Fennica *as it left Portland, Oregon.*

The walrus bull slacks atop his floe, tusks
out at an angle self-satisfied, gazing down
through whiskers at the fragrant mounds
of sunning female blubber lying heaped
about his flippers. The sotted monarch's
barge drifts on through walrine dreams,
slow as the lazy solar dip toward ocean
marking midnight for this court of snores.
Almost hot, the light, but the royal pinniped
is not moved to stir. Hard enough to find
a seat for summer's throne; pleasure's
pinnacle teeters on the roll of one or two
degrees. One eye gleams, slitted in survey
of voluptuous domain. No disquiet rules
him. The sea is orca-dark below the green.
Short-sighted king! O hapless queens!

THE MILKY WAY IN L.A.
Based on a true story
Keith Gaboury

A blackout is shackling
city light citizens

as emergency dispatchers
steep their teas

under the bombardment
of neighbors calling in, perplexed

over a strange glowing cloud
hovering in menace:

the Milky Way's
neurological connectivity

synchronized
into a Frankensteinian creature
alive on Sunset Boulevard,

dethroning the Hollywood
glare bomb from its perch
in a celebrity high-rise.

In one-story enclaves,
familias and families
gape at the gut punch of a sky

draped across a concrete sprawl
where an urbanite is lost
in the neighborhood of her birth,

a black root darkness
spilling
into the maternity ward's glow.

SOFT

Linda Parsons

I am soft. Soft as the fatted calf the prodigal

comes home to. Soft as the corona of fat

ringing the pâté Christophe served in my rose-

hung gîte. Soft with le canard, scored, seared

in honey, balsamic, shallots. My thighs soft

with Roquefort, marbled in all the tender places,

languished in Deep France without squats

on waking to work. Soft as cobbles

along the Way of St. James, pilgrims winding

narrows to Santiago de Compostela. Soft

as millet wheeled to Sunday market, Auvillar's

baskets of coquilles, macaroons, fleur de sel.

Centuries soft in alcoves, the must of L'église

Saint-Pierre, porcelain tributes to beloveds,

my reach through time's gray veil. My knees

soft in daily descent past the old convent

to write nothing soft, nothing limping,

to strop lines, hammer to a sheen. Light falls

on my knapsack, soft as the callas in high May.

This camino a weightless field of stars

at the confluence of country and river.

The Garonne braids the Tennessee,

a ribbon lacing Pyrenees to Appalachians,

uphill and down, this daughter wandered far.

HESITATING FRACTIONS

Cristina J. Baptista

Bravery is mysterious as a penny in the hull,
like the first man volunteering to try out
the modern bulletproof vest. Something rattles in the ribs,
in the belly. W. H. Murphy held out

hope like casually draping laundry on a line,
expecting to take it down later. Less than ten feet away,
a gun could have done anything
in September 1923.

He may have thought,
do what you do with grace and form—people are watching!
Just don't expect anyone to remember.
Everyone, as it would turn out, also forgot Fred Noonan.

Filippo Negroli tried it first, in 1538. Of course,
nothing is a new idea, although we often pretend to not see,
more dazzled by damascening, forgetting its practicality.
Even now, a Western comes on and people watch

because it's John Wayne whose name is billed,
who plays the star-packer, who puffs an impressive chest
and makes an impressive chase—but I can't help it.
I spy Yakima Canutt and won't pretend no one can tell it's him.

Nerve means never unraveling,
a cloth caught on a loosened nail that has to tug out
instead of gently let things go. Pluck, audacity—
a determined sense of knowing no one will know.

In Washington D.C., it wasn't Murphy who kept the slug,
nor the vest—having swallowed it. Deputy Sheriff
Charles W. Smith was given the bullet as a souvenir,
though it was Murphy who took the risk,

who "never batted an eye," as witnesses claimed. Eleven pounds
of protective wear and a bullet tucked close to his mortality,
and he was left as he had begun: with nothing
but oppressed shaking and his life. But both men

must have been hesitating fractions surveying infinity.
They must have listened for that moment, as before the match strikes
a wick; and the wick, dry as Adam's skin,
thirsts for a single touch to be alive.

Courage:
it must come naturally slow,
like the perfect skin of ice healing itself
after the cutter has trampled and charged.

LAWN CARE

Paul Beilstein

Across the hedgerow, her neighbor's arms
tense up, his dull shears attack the overgrowth.

He doesn't want to hear this season's pairings:
begonias for goldfinches, potatoes for potato beetles...

He thinks she's the type who buys
whatever sounds good at the lawn and garden superstore. Last year,

the rhododendron.
She summoned him to the plant,

hummed those four leafy syllables.
Rhododendron.

When she lifted a browning petal
to look at it with its others once more before

plucking it
and dropping it into her bucket,

he thought of his mother
in her casket

before it was shut
and she was lowered

and he put down his shears and swore off yard work for a while.
Anyway,

he hates her hummingbird feeder,
hung from a crookneck iron bar rising out of the hyacinths,

and his arms were tired,
and it was lunch time.

The other neighbor, across her firewood pyramid,
plays cool.

He would give his lungs to know how she does it, how she makes
all those incompatible plants

grow in one backyard.
He mows his lawn with a method:

this week front-to-back,
next week diagonal.

CROWS DIE TOO

Kevin McCarthy

So common as to be
invisible, yet the sky
would be inconsolable
without the croaky ink
darts, beaky frolics,
skulking jeers, the
signs from beyond

In a dense Colorado
forest, a slaloming
shadow peers over a
wing and piles into
a pine, dead instantly,
no wry comrade knowing,
no kin to poke liquid
obsidian remains

In a tall Seattle
park, a death watch – the
wayfaring sage squatting
in grass under evergreens
studded with ebon apostles,
no mock or gibe tendered

All those wise guys with
nothing to say

DEUTERONOMY 23:2

Djelloul Marbrook

No one born of a forbidden union may enter the assembly of the Lord.
Even to the tenth generation, none of his descendants...

It took a wile or two and even then
it was hard to get a mechanic's purchase
on bastardy as transfiguration, but when he did
he emerged from the King James whole
not belonging to anyone, not longing
to enter into the conjugation of one damned thing,
a rogue cell in the body politic, an anarchist
who thought of flags as diapers.
Glorious bastardy, sinistral, sinister,
a threat to the authorized version of events,
a backwards storyteller, nonsense jabberer,
on the outs, mooning insiders through their thermopains.
But it wasn't easy, it was a sandhogger's job
clearing the tunnel between the eye and the brain,
and another kind of job convincing the brain
to live with the evidence.

DREAM WITNESS

Marilyn Kallet

After the Goodfella wasted me
I played dead. The thug
swaggered like a ham actor,
Soprano understudy.
Now he's plugging
Chik-fil-A.

At last, my turn
to grill the witness:
"Why shoot me?"
We aimed to nail you
when you were young,
when your father
ratted on Joey Gallo
about vending machines
and phone threats.
Fucking wiretaps!
Then bullets
at Umberto's Clam House.

"So? Why send an actor
to whack me
after all these years?"
Crime's an art, too,
Sweetheart.
Some art is a crime.
"Not mine, I hope?"
You know best what's
 malformed.

Maybe playing dead
is my crime?
Rise, timid poet!

The Goodfella gets paid scale.
He'll go home,
put his feet up.
Write on louder,
blare like a
brass band. Behind you
marches the house band,

Benny G and
Louie Armstrong,
still knocking 'em dead.
Maybe Joy Harjo will
back you live on sax.
You breathe, you play,
belt out a new song.
Your choice, doll.
Your parade.

"Yes, but how are you different
from the gangsters?"
an academic asked.
"I don't stalk little girls
on the way home
from school.
Don't murder,
don't own a gun.
I write love poems,
not to Joey Gallo.
Leave that to Bobby Dylan.

I don't threaten
anyone,
not at my age.
No animals were smoked
in the making
of this poem."

FOG MADE OF IRON

Linda Nemec Foster

> "The universe really
> is a weird place."
>
> —Alan Boss

OK, listen to this.
Astronomers just discovered
a planet that is so airy
it has the density
of Styrofoam. And
somewhere else
there's a planet
where the surface
temperature reaches
3100 degrees,
where the gray fog
is so dense
it's made of iron.
Imagine the irony
of iron raindrops,
my daughter
nonchalantly posits
as she stirs her coffee.

I respond with a simple
nod. Yes, I can
imagine this universe
of irony where daughters
turn from students to teachers,
where mothers turn
from lectures to silence,
where even the sun
turns on its axis without
holding on. And the sky
must release every
cloud to become blue,
blue, pure blue
before the dark night
can release any star.
Those small lights
that outline Cassiopeia
and her Andromeda.

250

THE SULTAN'S TENT

Brandon Marlon

Veiled belly dancers gyrated,
delighting patron and guests
gorging on lamb and olives,
rosemary flecks in their teeth.

Feathery fronds spun awhirl
as squirming houris charmed
between swipes at matbucha
or nips of steaming mint tea.

Awaiting sizzling shish taouk,
emirs traded caravan hearsay,
fiercely rivaling one another
with reports of desert ghouls.

Yet within the host's soul,
a quest for insight stirred,
diverting regal attentions
from tinkling waist belts.

Concerned with obscurities,
he forsook canopied luxury,
envious of unconfined stars,
keen to fathom their secrets.

A LOVE STORY

Carolyn Evans Campbell

We crawled out of the sea,
wet, blinking,
emerged from the mud
to dry in the sun,
lose our scales,
fashion fur.

I hid under the leaves,
watched you stand
and stretch into a little god,
listened to you
sing forth the stars,
open your great heart
to roar back the thunder,
and I followed you

rocking the seeds of civilization
in my pelvis, pulling
slippery golden grasses
between my fingers,
poking blossoms, open
and red as mouths,
into my hair.

In our night nest
of crushed flowers, pollen,
sweet minty leaves, and
our pungent nakedness,
the earth moved with
my spread, my arch,
my mount and moan,
my salt,
your salt,
your surge,
your silver trails.

And when you slept
like a sea snail coiled,
I listened
to the ocean in you
and the pulse of the universe
in your chest.
I ran my tongue and fingers
over your landscape and
the horizon of your belly
and waited for the morning
to strike you crimson.
And I followed you.

I watched you capture
the lightning in your fists,
force the winding rivers
into straight lines,
carry the mountains on your back,
tear them down stone by stone
and erect them into monuments.
When you cursed the elements
for standing in your way,
I trembled.

Hidden in the day
and in the secrets of night,
I watched you wail with the wind,
leap with flames, chant
the fire song, eat the earth,
adorn yourself
with red and ochre clay.
I saw you silenced by the evening star,
the night full of moon,
the lift of loons off the lake.

I watched you swallow the sun
and glow with its heat,
and when you blew your warm
breath around a frozen wren
to spark it back to life,
Oh, how I loved you.

XOXO

Notes on
Contributors

Thank you

Cristina J. Baptista is a Portuguese-American writer and English teacher from Connecticut. Her work has appeared in *Structo, The Cortland Review, CURA*, and elsewhere. She holds a Ph.D. in English from Fordham University, and documented the 38th Voyage of the Charles W. Morgan, the world's last wooden whaleship, through poetry.

Patricia Barone is the author of *The Scent of Water* from Blue Light Press, and *The Wind,* and *Handmade Paper* from New Rivers Press.

Claire Bateman's bio can be found on page 28.

Paul Beilstein was born and raised in Springfield, Illinois. He took the long way through California and Oregon to arrive in Champaign, Illinois, where he currently lives with his wife, Shereen.

Lynne Burnett lives in West Vancouver, B.C. with her husband. Publications include *North Shore Magazine, CV2, Geist,* the *Pedestal Magazine, Malahat Review, Calyx, Modern Haiku, Pandora's Collective,* and *New Millennium Writings*. In 2011, she was shortlisted for both Arc's Poem of the Year and the Bridport Prize; in 2012, for both the New Letters Poem of the Year and the Bridport Prize, and also placed in several contests. She has self-published one chapbook, *Stealing Eternity*.

Carolyn Evans Campbell is a teacher, writer, poet, and artist in Evergreen, Colorado and the Denver region. She has received national acclaim for six books of poetry, a novel, and a memoir. "The creative journey with other writers and artists is joy beyond words."

Alexis Williams Carr has been a part of *NMW* since its founding in 1996, first as a humble envelope stuffer and errand-runner, before working her way up to entry screener, then assistant editor.

She graduated Magna Cum Laude from Middle Tennessee State University with a BA in English Literature.

After working in higher education and in corporate communications and publishing, Alexis was thrilled to take over as Editor of *New Millennium Writings* in 2012.

She has to date published hundreds of writers within the pages of *NMW* and looks forward to many more years of rewarding and publishing members of the writing community.

Brent A. Carr earned his bachelor's degree at the University of Tennessee, where he studied psychology and botany and worked for the university newspaper, *The Daily Beacon*, and the *Phoenix Literary Arts Magazine*. As a designer and Associate Publisher for *NMW*, he finds purpose and inspiration in the words of the late bard and mystic, Terence McKenna: "The artist's task is to save the soul of mankind; and anything less is a dithering while Rome burns. Because of the artists, who are self-selected, for being able to journey into the Other, if the artists cannot find the way, then the way cannot be found."

Robert S. Carr is a native of Orlando, Florida, and winner of the *NMW* 20th Poetry Prize (2006). A graduate of Vanderbilt and the University of Central Florida, he teaches secondary-school students with learning challenges and is also a musical entertainer. Robert is married to DeAnn Lovering, and their son, Michael, is a graduate student at Columbia University.

Mary Davies Cole, poet and contemporary artist, writes and paints about the confluence of nature, time, and memory. A retired art therapist and teacher, she lives in Massachusetts with her husband, two retrievers, and a lot of poems and canvas. This is her second poem in *New Millennium Writings*. She is also published in *A Feast of Cape Ann Poets*.

Doris Ivie relishes her retirement from a lifetime of "professing," reads broadly, cultivates choiceless awareness, teaches an online personal growth course, and values above all other experiences her three "sits" with the Dalai Lama. Doris co-edited two East Tennessee regional literary anthologies: *Breathing the Same Air* and *A Tapestry of Voices*.

Linda Nemec Foster is the author of nine collections of poetry, including *Amber Necklace from Gdansk* from LSU Press, and *Talking Diamonds* from New Issues Press. Her work has been published in *The Georgia Review*, *New American Writing*, *North American Review*, and nominated for the Pushcart Prize. A new chapbook, *The Elusive Heroine: My Daughter Lost in Magritte*, is forthcoming from Cervena Barva Press.

Keith Gaboury grew up in Kansas but abhors farms. Like his first crush, *The Paris Review* recently rejected him. Keith earned an MFA in creative writing from Emerson College. He now writes poetry in Cambridge, Massachusetts while making a go as a pre-k teacher.

Hedy Habra has authored two poetry collections, *Under Brushstrokes*, finalist for the USA Best Book Award and for the International Book Award, and *Tea in Heliopolis*, winner of the USA Best Book Award. Her work appears in *Cimarron Review*, *Bitter Oleander*, *Gargoyle*, *Nimrod*, *Poet Lore*, *World Literature Today*, and *Verse Daily*.

Anca Hariton—for her, writing is delivering. It matured and diversified after she immigrated to the U.S. from Eastern Europe. It brought her recognition (a collaborative grant), and publication in poetry magazines and picture books, moving now to the forefront of her artwork at *SacristimaStudio.com*.

Georganne Harmon's poems have appeared in literary journals and her chapbook, *We Will Have Ghosts*. She has recently completed her first novel.

Linda Lee Harper's *Kiss, Kiss* won the Cleveland State University Poetry Center's Open Competition, and her first collection, *Toward Desire*, won the Washington Prize. Of her eight chapbooks, the newest is *Quake,* from Finishing Line Press, and another favorite is *Blue Flute*, from Adastra Press.

Clarinda Harriss, a professor emerita of English at Towson University and publisher/editor of BrickHouse Books, Inc., is the co-author of a booklength translation of *The Pearl,* and of *Hot Sonnets: An Anthology.* She is the author of six published poetry collections. Her most recently published book is *The White Rail*, a short-story collection. She has worked with prison writers for decades.

Matt Hohner holds an MFA in Writing and Poetics from Naropa University in Boulder, Colorado. A finalist for the Ballymaloe International Poetry Prize and *Cobalt's* Earl Weaver Baseball Writing Prize, Hohner recently took both third and first prizes in the Maryland Writers Association Poetry Awards. He lives in Baltimore, Maryland.

Karen Hunt's bio can be found on page 92.

Marilyn Kallet is the author of seventeen books, including *The Love That Moves Me*, poetry from Black Widow Press. She has translated Paul Eluard's *Last Love Poems*, Péret's *The Big Game*, and co-translated Chantal Bizzini's *Disenchanted City*. Dr. Kallet is Nancy Moore Goslee Professor of English at the University of Tennessee. She also leads poetry workshops for VCCA-France in Auvillar. She has performed her poems on campuses and in theaters across the United States as well as in France and Poland, as a guest of the U.S. Embassy's "America Presents" program. The University of Tennessee lists her as an expert on poetry's role in times of crisis.

C. Ann Kodra, an independent editor in Knoxville, Tennessee, has poems and short stories published in *Blueline, Gingerbread House, Memoir Journal, MOTIF, NMW, Now & Then, Prime Mincer, Yemassee, RHINO, Still: The Journal,* and others. She has served as a guest poetry editor for *The Medulla Review.*

Ellen LaFleche has published three chapbooks and was awarded The Ruth Stone Poetry Prize, the Philbrick Poetry Prize, and the Joe Gouveia Outermost Poetry Prize, among others. She is the assistant judge of the North Street Book Prize at *winningwriters.com.*

Jo Christiane Ledakis traveled the world as an international conference interpreter, lending her voice to many, from hog farmers to heart surgeons to heads of state. Her adventure of freeing her voice awaits publication. She captures the magic of life in poems and short stories and is thrilled to appear again in *NMW.*

Sandy Longley is an Associate Professor of English at Columbia-Greene Community College in Hudson, New York. Recent publications include *Spillway, The Nimrod Journal, Passager, Southword Journal,* and *The Naugatuck River Review.*

Alison Luterman is the author of three books of poetry: *The Largest Possible Life, See How We Almost Fly*, and *Desire Zoo. www.alisonluterman.net*

Djelloul Marbrook has written five books of fiction and four of poetry, including *Far from Algiers* (2008, Kent State University Press), winner of the Wick Poetry Prize and the 2010 International Book Award (poetry). Scheduled from Leaky Boot (UK) in 2017 are five books of poetry and five of fiction.

Brandon Marlon is a writer from Ottawa, Canada. He received his BA in Drama and English from the University of Toronto and his MA in English from the University of Victoria. His poetry was awarded the Harry Hoyt Lacey Prize in Poetry (Fall 2015), and his writing has been published in more than 150 publications in twenty-three countries. *www.brandonmarlon.com*

Jackie Davis Martin's bio can be found on page 46.

Tim Mayo's poems and reviews have appeared in *Barrow Street, Poetry International, Poet Lore, River Styx, Salamander, San Pedro River Review, Tar River Poetry, Verse Daily,* and *The Writer's Almanac.* His collection, *The Kingdom of Possibilities,* was published by Mayapple Press in 2009. He's a four-time Pushcart Prize Nominee and has been a top finalist for the annual Paumanok Award.

Kevin McCarthy is a Colorado poet, dramatist, essayist, and geologist. His early poems were well-received, but he didn't return to poetry until the recent death of a friend. Since 2012, seventeen of his poems have appeared in various journals, including *Neat, Common Ground, Review, Southwestern American Literature,* and *Written River.* "Enough Sky" was commended in The Poetry Society's 2014 National Competition.

Berwyn Moore's collections are *O Body Swayed* and *Dissolution of Ghosts,* both from Cherry Grove Collections. She was appointed Erie County, Pennsylvania's first poet laureate in 2009. Her poems have won awards from *Bellevue Literary Review, The Pinch Journal, Margie,* and *Negative Capability* and have appeared in *The Southern Review, Poetry Northwest, Nimrod, JAMA, Measure, Cimarron Review,* and others. She teaches at Gannon University in Erie, Pennsylvania.

Barbara Mossberg, President Emerita Goddard College, City Poet Emerita Pacific Grove, and Professor of Practice, Clark Honors College, University of Oregon, is a prize-winning poet, critic (*Emily Dickinson* was *Choice* Outstanding Academic Book of the Year), and professor who is devoted to poetry in civic life, as an actor, dramaturg, host of a weeky hour radio show (*The Poetry Slow Down*), and performer in Flash Mobs, You Tube, lit crawls, poetry slams, dramas, fundraising, readings, and TV. Her most recent book is with the New Women's Voices Series with Finishing Line Press, *Sometimes the Woman in the Mirror Is Not You (and Other Hopeful News Postings).*

Susan Nathiel's bio can be found on page 114.

Shelley Kitchura Nelson is enlightened by words and the natural world. She finds truth in moments as simple as a bird resting on her mare's back, to the chaos of a flooding river. Poetry offers this freelance writer and multitasker clarity for her stories. Her most recent publication appeared in *Pilgrimage*.

Emily Pittman Newberry's writing explores the challenges of living as spiritual beings in a material world. OneSpirit Press published two of her books; she wrote the poetry for the artist Shu-Ju Wang's artist's book, *Water,* and she was nominated for a Pushcart Prize in 2014. *www.butterflyarose.com*

Linda Parsons's bio can be found on page 138.

Elaine Pentaleri lives on twenty-two acres of field, woodland, and stream in Vermont. She is an education administrator, word player, wife, and mother of two daughters. Elaine has a particular interest in performance poetry and teaching poetry to children. Her poetry has appeared in a variety of small press publications.

Sashana Kane Proctor wrote stories in grammar school. Later she married, raised sons, worked as a teacher and gallery director, wrote poetry, divorced, journaled, worked in drug and alcohol treatment, found her lover, learned medical transcription, wrote lyric essays, retired, and here she is, writing in the redwoods.

Linwood Rumney's poems, nonfiction essays, and translations have appeared in *North American Review*, *Ploughshares*, *Crab Orchard Review*, *Puerto del Sol*, *Southern Review*, *Kenyon Review*, *Adirondack Review*, and elsewhere. An editorial assistant for Black Lawrence Press, he lives in Cincinnati, where he is pursuing a Ph.D.

Robert A. B. Sawyer is author of *AMERICAN LULLABY*, from Exits but No Escapes Press, NYC (2014). He was a winner of the 2003 *Discovery/The Nation Poetry Competition*, and has had poems in *Margie: The Journal of American Poetry, The Nation,* and *Jazz 2.* His poem, "How I Know She's Coming Home," was selected by Natasha Trethewey for *Meridian Best New Poets* 2007, and "Hong Kong Harbor 1984" became the lyrics to a choral piece composed by Philip White, which premiered in Los Angeles, by Angel City Chorale, June 2, 2012. (Renamed "On This Side of the Window," the poem/music was published by Santa Barbara Music Publishing, Inc., and performed May 11, 2015, by the Los Angeles Master Chorale Chamber Singers.) Sawyer has published a short story in *Adbuster*, a critical article in *Afterimage, The Journal of Media Arts and Cultural Criticism*, and an Op-Ed piece in *The New York Times*.

Eric St. Clair published short stories and magazine articles. He also worked as a statistician, social worker, horticulturist, and a laboratory assistant. [*Following a year-long search, beginning on October 25, 2015, St. Clair's story herein has been deemed orphaned. A documented history of the search to identify the author's heir or estate representative has established that a good-faith effort has been made.*]

Annie Stenzel's poems appear in both print and online journals, including *Quiddity, Ambit, Catamaran Literary Reader*, and *Lunch Ticket*. Her work has twice been nominated for a Pushcart Prize. She is also a letterpress printer, never happier than when her hands are covered in ink.

Noah Stetzer's bio can be found on page 24.

Laura Still is a poet, playwright, writer, and teller of local history stories for her tour business, Knoxville Walking Tours. Her poetry collection, *Guardians*, was released in 2009 by Celtic Cat Publishing and was followed in 2010 by *Acts of the Apostles, Vol. I*, a book of children's plays.

Jim Glenn Thatcher is a poet with work—and recognitions for his work—in a wide variety of publications. He has been submitting poems to *NMW*'s bi-annual contests since Summer 2010, when he won the First Place Poetry Prize for "Interlinear," a poem in which Nature tells its own story through a winter night and into dawn. In the *NMW* competitions since then, he's won one more (shared) First Place—"Understory"—and several Honorable Mentions. He teaches at Southern Maine Community College.

Armin Tolentino received his MFA in poetry at Rutgers University in Newark, New Jersey. His poetry has appeared, or is forthcoming, in *Mason's Road, The Bear Deluxe*, and *Blue Earth Review*. He was a 2014 Oregon Literary Arts Fellowship recipient.

Nina Varela's bio can be found on page 70.

Arne Weingart lives in Chicago, Illinois, where he is the principal of a graphic design firm specializing in identity and wayfinding. His work has been nominated for a Pushcart Prize and his book, *Levitation For Agnostics*, was the winner of the 2014 New American Press Poetry Prize.

Alexander Weinstein's bio can be found on page 32.

Ingrid Wendt, a Eugene, Oregon poet, is the author of five award-winning books of poems and co-editor of two anthologies. A musician by avocation, she and her husband, writer Ralph Salisbury, still own their modest vacation rental on the Oregon coast. Her brain tumor has been successfully removed. *www.ingridwendt.com*

Shanna Yetman's bio can be found on page 40.

$8,000 IN CASH PRIZES EACH YEAR

1. Categories: Poetry, Fiction, Flash Fiction, Nonfiction
2. $1,000 award plus publication for each category
3. Multiple and simultaneous submissions welcome
4. **No restrictions** on style or subject matter
5. *Anonymous judging*

ONLINE SUBMISSIONS

MAIL/POSTAL SUBMISSIONS

ADDITIONAL GUIDELINES

NONCONTEST SUBMISSIONS

PLEASE VISIT:

www.newmillenniumwritings.org

CONSECUTIVE WRITING CONTESTS	WRITERS AND POETS PUBLISHED	ANTHOLOGIES DELIVERED	AWARDED TO WRITERS AND POETS
43	**1,600+**	**50,000+**	**$200,000+**

newmillenniumwritings.org

Made in the USA
Charleston, SC
28 February 2017